OFF THE BEATEN TRACK

OFF THE BEATEN TRACK

20 multi-day walks on New Zealand farm and backcountry tracks

Colin Moore

craig potton publishing

ACKNOWLEDGEMENTS

This book was only possible because of the generous help of the track operators. They willingly gave their time to guide me over the tracks and spoke openly and honestly about their passions and those aspects of the past and present most dear to them.

Their clients, whom I met on various walks, were equally generous of their time; their spirit invariably imbued with the bonhomie that comes from having a good time in a good place.

The track operators also made available their personal and publicity photographs for selection and free of copyright. Photojournalist colleagues—Alistair Hall, Shaun Barnett, Tony Gates and John Rhodes—also generously provided crucial photographs.

The pioneering guidebook to 'private' walks, *Hidden Trails* by Walter Hirsh, was of invaluable help in understanding the nature of the treks.

None of this help would have been to any avail, however, had not Renée Lang, of Renaissance Publishing, conceived the idea for this book and, to my good fortune, asked me to write it, and Jane Connor, of Craig Potton Publishing, accepted the manuscript for publication. I am also indebted to Caroline Budge, CPP Production Editor, for tidying my copy, and designer Tina Delceg for turning the concept into reality.

Finally, my family need not remind me that this project would not have been completed without their unstinting support and patience.

PHOTO CREDITS

Colin Moore, Redactor Services; Shaun Barnett, Black Robin Photography; Tony Gates, Leatherwood Lenz; Kerry Walker Photography; Kerry Fox, Photofox; Alistair Hall; John Rhodes; Wayne Baxter; Tony Bouzaid; Chris and Louise Kay; Peter MacIntyre; Sue and Mason Fraser; Sonia Inder; Dayle Lakeman; Simon Harvey; Sally Handyside; Jo McAtamney; Colin Monteath; Kylee Simpson; Nick Clark; Tuatara Tours NZ Ltd; Tuatapere Hump Track Ltd; Craig Potton; Department of Conservation.

First published in 2009 by Craig Potton Publishing

Craig Potton Publishing
98 Vickerman Street, PO Box 555, Nelson, New Zealand
www.craigpotton.co.nz

© Maps by GeographX

© Photography: Individual photographers
© Text: Colin Moore

ISBN 978 1 877517 04 4

Printed in China by 1010 Printing International Ltd

This book is copyright. Apart from any fair dealing for the purposes of private study, research, criticism or review, as permitted under the Copyright Act, no part may be reproduced by any process without the permission of the publishers.

CONTENTS

Acknowledgements ... 4
Introduction ... 7

NORTH ISLAND WALKS

1. Home is the sailor—Glenfern Sanctuary walks, Great Barrier Island ... 10
2. Roaming in the gloaming—Dundle Hill Walk, Waitomo, King Country ... 20
3. Luxury, sheer luxury—Walk Gisborne, Gisborne ... 30
4. Footprints on a canvas—Whana Walk, Hawke's Bay ... 40
5. The answer lies in the soil—Walk Westridge, Ongarue, near Taumarunui ... 50
6. Down to the wallow—Eastern Taranaki Experience, Stratford ... 60
7. Tongariro trumped—Tongariro Alpine Crossing and other walks in Tongariro National Park ... 70
8. A river runs through it—Kawhatau Valley Walk, Mangaweka ... 80
9. Farmstay comfort—Weka Walks, Mt Huia farm, Ruahine Road, Mangaweka ... 90
10. Taming the Tararuas—Tararua Walk, Masterton, Wairarapa ... 100
11. Marching on its stomach—Tora Coastal Walk, South Wairarapa ... 110

SOUTH ISLAND WALKS

12. Captured by the Cape—Cape Campbell Walkway, Ward, Marlborough ... 120
13. Golden vintage—Awatere Tussock Track, Marlborough ... 130
14. Whale of a walk—Kaikoura Coast Track, North Canterbury ... 140
15. Home, sweet home—Hurunui High Country Track, Hurunui, North Canterbury ... 150
16. In the beginning—Banks Peninsula Track, Akaroa, Canterbury ... 160
17. Island time—The Akaroa Walk, Banks Peninsula, Canterbury ... 170
18. Walking in space—Glenthorne Station High Country Walks, Lake Coleridge ... 180
19. Heart of the high country—Four Peaks High Country Track, Geraldine, South Canterbury ... 190
20. On nature's edge—Hump Ridge Track, Tuatapere, Southland ... 200

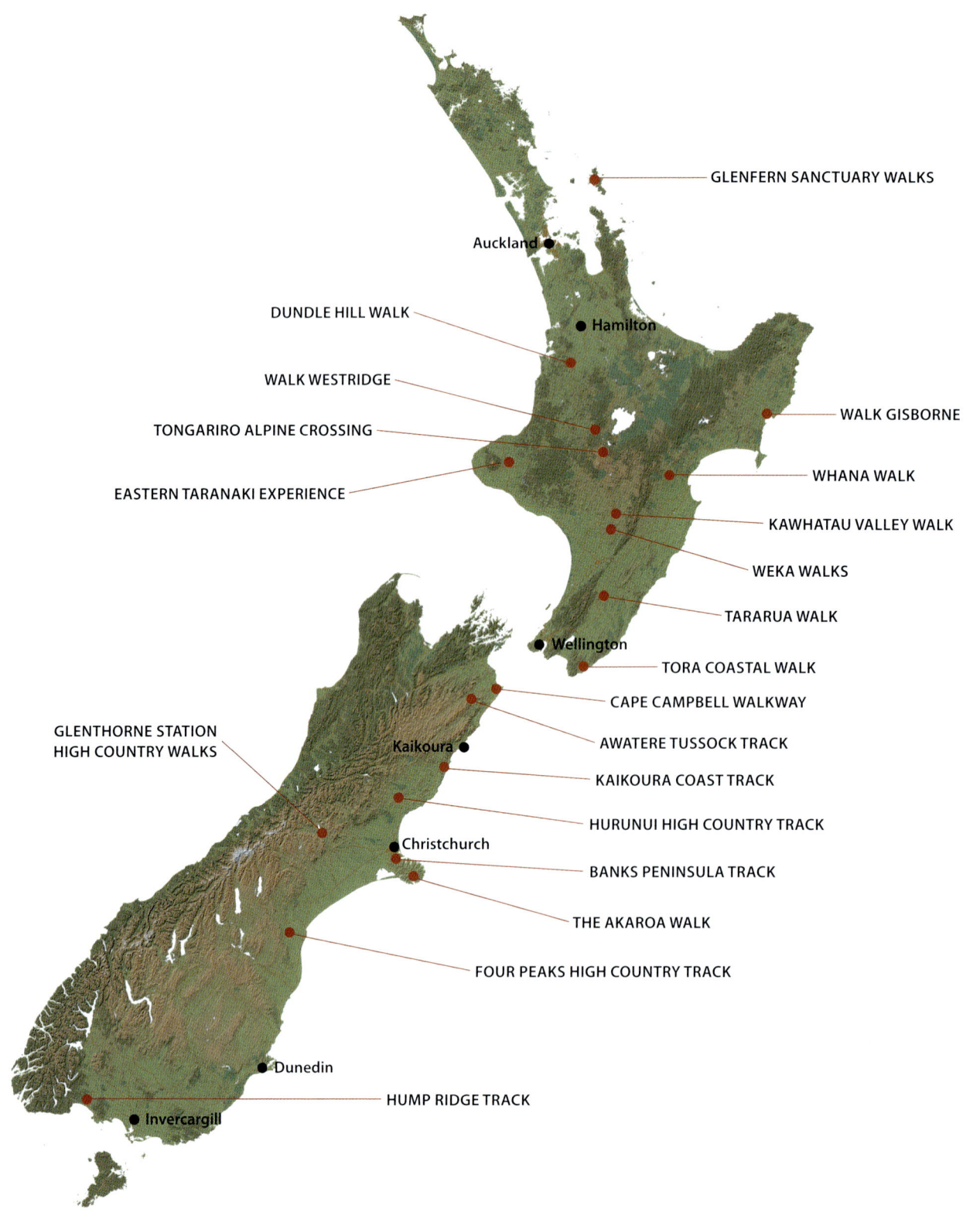

INTRODUCTION

In the early 1980s New Zealand underwent enormous change as the fourth Labour Government threw the country into the global economy with a raft of startling economic reforms. Under the aegis of 'levelling the playing field' in the cause of economic efficiency, decades of regulation, protection and subsidy were mercilessly ejected in favour of the new disciplines of free market, user pays, competition and cost visibility.

Nothing was immune from the reforms, including outdoor recreation and the national psyche, although the effect of Rogernomics on the latter was rarely acknowledged.

For many lovers of the outdoors, the realisation of the new order came when the Department of Conservation, working under the same strictures as the rest of the public sector, introduced an overnight fee on its backcountry huts. It was an unheard of break with cherished backcountry tradition and ethic. Much of the hut network owed its existence to voluntary labour and the communal spirit that, at least in the outdoors, no man was an island entire of itself. The unthinkable, an entry fee for National and Forest Parks, seemed certain to follow—and there were many economic reformists pressing for just that.

However, a more significant demonstration of the changes being wrought on the nation with all the subtlety of a wrecking ball, was the opening in December 1989 of a private walking track on Banks Peninsula. Those Cantabrians who had sailed from Britain the previous century to a land where Jack was as good as his Master, where there was no such thing as private fishing waters, and where public access along the margins of river and sea was guaranteed by royal decree, would surely roll with distress in their graves.

If the end wasn't nigh, it was certainly so for life in New Zealand as we had known it until then. It seemed that, almost overnight, a monetary value had been attached to everything, including those practices we had long cherished and considered to be part of our birthright as New Zealanders. Property, land included, was now fiercely private. Years later, in a discussion with some farmers, I found no better example of the 1980s change to our national psyche than in their attitude towards the humble field mushroom that pops up in paddocks every year around Easter.

In the 1950s it was a family treat to drive into the country to gather mushrooms. You would spot them near the road in a paddock with no obvious or nearby sign of life or ownership, climb the fence and fill your basket, all without so much as a nervous backward glance or guilty thought. If not picked, the mushrooms would soon die. We sometimes picked blackberries in much the same way. Well, not any more because, as my farmer friends indignantly insisted, that was theft from private property and better the mushrooms die than be taken without permission or payment. Of course, my parents were originally country folk and would have sought permission if there had been a farmhouse nearby, but I don't think they considered themselves to be poachers when there wasn't one.

Yet change always seems transitory, at least in its

perception. What was once startling soon becomes accepted as commonplace. So backcountry hut users now turn their hut fee angst on those users who don't buy hut tickets, 'private' tracks and 'guided' walks are now an integral and much welcomed part of the panoply of outdoor recreation options—and those mushrooms no longer grow so profusely, anyway; killed off, perhaps, by more 'efficient' farm practices.

And for all the fundamental changes to our economy and national psyche, one thing seems to remain pretty much the same for both. Farmers are still the backbone of the New Zealand economy and they retain the characteristics that in essence, town or country, we like to think of as typically New Zealand. They work hard but play hard too, are somewhat conservative yet innovative, are down to earth but comfortable rubbing shoulders with anyone, have a dry sense of humour, and a well of integrity, honesty and generosity. This book is essentially about them.

As it transpires, our so-called 'private' tracks are nothing at all like those private fishing waters of Britain. They were places reserved by the privileged for the privileged. New Zealand's private walks arose neither from greed nor cynicism, but because farmers facing the winds of economic change had to diversify. So they began to farm people.

But that is only part of the story because these landowners invariably have a sense of history and an innate feeling for the land and want to share it with other people. Who knows how history might one day judge the advent of 'private' walks, but there seems to have been a certain serendipity about it.

By the 1980s those hearty folk of the outdoors who built tracks and huts in the wilderness and preferred to take their recreation under the umbrella of a club, were fast disappearing, with or without economic reforms. Those who took their recreation in the outdoors in the last decades of the twentieth century tended to have greater expectations and less time with which to fulfil them. Better to set off with a few mates and pay DOC's hut fees than spend time in communal building activity.

The trend coincided with the arrival of older folk who still aspired to the hills but no longer wanted to lug a heavy burden, sleep too rough, or live on hard tack.

In short, in 1989 those Banks Peninsula farmers not only created a way to take pressure off their economic problems without selling the family silver, but tapped into a germinating market and a trend about to unfurl.

And at almost the same time, the decades-old movement of young New Zealanders spending time abroad on their OE (overseas experience) began to reverse. Tourists not afraid to dirty their boots came looking for clean and green New Zealand.

Of course, walkers who take to the tracks featured in this book are nowhere near all old locals or young foreigners. They are the sort of eclectic mix you would expect to find anywhere in the outdoors. But generally, they do have in common a desire for some creature comforts, the restraints of time that demand some things be organised for them—and an overwhelming commitment to see the New Zealand backcountry.

The private walk operators provide all that, as well as an insight into other aspects of the backcountry that are not found on tracks in our National and Forest Parks. There is a lot more to the outdoors than native bush.

When first approached to write this book I worried that many of the walks would be pretty much the same—one farm paddock after another. The reality proved to be far different. Each walk has its own distinctive characteristic. Some focus on coastal views, others on the subalpine high country. Some have large blocks of native bush while others are treks over rolling tussockland. On these walks you will find rivers where trout feed quietly in the pools, penguin chicks in a nest by a track, seal pups in a sea cave nursery, ghost towns that once housed hundreds of timber workers, limestone caves, and a sense of history in almost every step.

Even in farming terms they are quite different, with no two farmers sharing the same views on stock or farm practice. It is part of the fascination of these walks to talk to the landowners and walk guides. Ignore the opportunity if it is presented and you ignore what sets these walks apart from a traditional tramping trip. These are people of the land and they are more than happy to share their knowledge with you.

One thing all the landowners have in common is a love of the land and a desire to see it protected in perpetuity. Most have retired areas from grazing to allow the regeneration of native bush and covenanted blocks of land to the Queen Elizabeth II Trust.

Not all walks featured here are over private land and so can hardly be described as 'private' tracks. What they share, however, is that in exchange for a modest number of dollars, some enterprising folk will take out much of the grunt from your day by carrying your pack and pampering you in the evening with a warm, comfy bed, and even a cooked meal if you want, all at a cost that compares more than favourably with backpacker hostel rates in cities or tourist towns.

As the hard-core trampers of the 1960s move into their pension entitlement years, and the baby boomer generation follows not far behind, the offer of a bit of comfort becomes increasingly tempting. Many of the folk sharing the pleasure of these walks have already stomped up and down most of the hardest hills in the New Zealand wilderness, carrying huge loads on their backs. Their spirit remains willing but their bodies are now grateful for a lesser load. And they are happy to seek out new and perhaps less demanding paths.

A particular feature of these walks is the innovative range of accommodation provided. Much of it belongs to a rural past; many of the huts and lodges deserve an Historic Places Trust listing, and all tend to make the evenings as much of a fascinating adventure as the day's walk to get there.

It is perhaps this feature, more than any other, that sets the private walks apart from a tramping trip in the public estate. Traditional New Zealand tramping, using an extensive network of basic backcountry huts, has no exact replica anywhere else in the world, whereas the network of private walks has similarities with inn-to-inn or farmhouse to farmhouse walking common in Europe.

But that it is not to suggest that New Zealand's walks on farmland and backcountry are anything but wholly New Zealand. From the kauri bush-fringed bays of Great Barrier Island to the soaring snow-capped peaks and open tussockland of Canterbury, these are classic New Zealand walks.

HOME IS THE SAILOR
GLENFERN SANCTUARY WALKS, GREAT BARRIER ISLAND

It is easy to imagine that God or nature created Port Fitzroy on Great Barrier Island for outdoor recreation. Just behind the harbour, with its numerous bays and inlets, rises the rugged volcanic spine of the fourth largest island in New Zealand, part of a mountain chain that once stretched from Northland to the Coromandel Peninsula.

The sculptured 627 metre heights of Mt Hobson (Hirakimata), its bluffs and pinnacles easily visible from anywhere in the harbour, are clothed in kauri forest—a tiny pocket that the rapacious loggers of last century couldn't reach. But the denuded land is slowly regenerating in native forest; the distinctive olive green cones of maturing kauri now break through the bush canopy. Many of the best bushwalking tracks in the 60 per cent of the 285 square kilometre island that is controlled by the Department of Conservation radiate from Fitzroy.

The extensive harbour is a maritime nirvana, a recreational gift from the melted water of the last ice age that drowned valleys and isolated the Barrier from the Coromandel and created the Hauraki Gulf. Pohutukawa unmolested by possums hang over a mostly rocky Fitzroy foreshore peppered with oysters and mussels, a natural fish nursery and a larder for sea birds. At the height of summer up to 1000 yachts, launches and large runabouts anchor in Port Fitzroy, some 70 kilometres across the Gulf from downtown Auckland—although you might be hard pressed to find many of them as they seek seclusion in the multitude of harbour anchorages. Fitzroy is a splendid natural harbour with its entrance neatly blocked by Kaikoura Island, the largest of the 23 islands dotted around the coast of the Barrier, leaving the narrow Man o' War Passage in the south and a slightly larger northern entrance.

Defence planners figured that the Japanese Empire would soon spot the strategic significance of a harbour with both a front and back door that was big enough to shelter a naval fleet, and they set up gun emplacements and a controlled minefield to keep any Japanese invaders out. What makes a good parking spot for a navy also makes a perfect anchorage for yachties, so it is hardly surprising that the late Sir Peter Blake called Great Barrier his 'favourite island in the whole world' and would frequently drop the pick in Fitzroy harbour. So, too, did another legend of New Zealand sailing, Tony Bouzaid. Long before New Zealand's involvement in the America's Cup, it was the Bouzaid family who were responsible for putting New Zealand on the international yachting charts.

The family yacht was the famous 1899 Logan sloop, *Rainbow I*, and with that pedigree behind him, Tony's brother

The North Island kaka is common, but endangered, on Great Barrier Island and its raucous screech and whistle is frequently heard in the Glenfern Sanctuary.

Chris won the international One Ton Cup with *Rainbow II*. The Bouzaids, whose family sail-making business was taken over by the huge American company Hood Sails, used to spend summer holidays moored at Port Fitzroy. Over the years Tony Bouzaid watched Fitzroy House, a splendid farmhouse built in 1901, fall to rack and ruin after it was left in trust to seven grandchildren who were scattered all over the world. The villa had a varied history, having been used as a summer guesthouse, with a dormitory block added in 1914—barged in two halves from Whangaparapara where it had been the single men's quarters for the Kauri Timber Company. A separate cottage was built on the site that the Bouzaid family used to rent during the school holidays.

Eventually Bouzaid's angst at the slow death of Fitzroy House led him and his wife Mal to buy the house in 1992, intending to use it as a holiday home that would be more extensively used in their retirement. Nine tradesmen worked on the restoration over 14 months. To restore it to its original design and remove rotten timber, the house had to be virtually rebuilt. The freight bill to get materials to the Barrier was $5000 a month. The Bouzaids moved into the home in November 1993 and decided to take advantage of a regular ferry service then running to Port Fitzroy by using part of the home as a backpackers' hostel and renting Seaview Cottage to family groups.

Then Bouzaid realised something was missing. He and his family had always walked the bush trails on Great Barrier, but they were now silent. The birdlife had gone. One cause was obvious—the place was rife with feral cats. He began trapping wild cats on his 83 hectare property, then set up bait stations to get rid of rats. Bouzaid also built tracks to maintain the grid of bait stations and began propagating

Port Fitzroy (left) is a haven for Auckland yachties but thanks to the conservation efforts of yachtsman Tony Bouzaid (above) and his wife Mal, it has also become a haven for wildlife. A 2 kilometre pest-proof fence across the Kotuku Peninsula (middle) protects birds in 230 hectares from rat and cat predation. The Unimog all-terrain vehicle (bottom) was bought from the Army by the Bouzaids and is now used to transport walkers.

native trees from island stock. As one thing led to another, Glenfern Sanctuary was born—a raucous private bird sanctuary with gullies of lush native bush and former pasture healthily regenerating into a forest. When Bouzaid found that his trapping was being undone by pests re-invading from neighbouring properties, he got permission to lay traps and bait stations on the entire 230 hectare peninsula that Glenfern Sanctuary sits on. But even with more than 500 rat bait stations it was difficult to ensure a perfectly safe haven, so the Bouzaids set up a charitable trust and raised funds to build a pest-proof fence across the base of the peninsula. A highlight of the Bouzaids' conservation efforts has been the reintroduction of the North Island robin in 2005. The birds, taken from the Tiritiri Matangi sanctuary, had been extinct on Great Barrier for 140 years.

All this is great news for bushwalkers because it means that Glenfern Sanctuary, 61 hectares of which is covenanted to the Queen Elizabeth II Trust, is likely to become home to such sensitive species as the kokako, kiwi, saddleback and tuatara. The backpackers' hostel is now used by sanctuary staff, but Seaview Cottage, built in the 1940s adjacent to the main house and fully renovated, is the base for the four-day walking programme that could be easily billed as the 'Best of the Barrier.'

On day one, after arriving from Auckland by boat or light plane and settling into Seaview Cottage, guests are rewarded with the first dramatic impressions of Fitzroy harbour from Sunset Rock, followed by a two-hour guided walk through the Glenfern Sanctuary. More than 10,000 native trees have been planted in the sanctuary to bring birdsong back to the area. A highlight is a 600-year-old kauri. Bouzaid has rigged a wire-rope suspension bridge

Seaview Cottage (above), once rented by the Bouzaid family as a school holiday retreat, is now used to accommodate visitors to Glenfern Sanctuary.

into the tree's crown so that people can get a bird's eye view of this forest giant. There is usually time to tackle an excellent short bush walk, the Old Lady Walk, that begins its loop near Fitzroy House, before following a stream through regenerating native forest and a delightful grove of old nikau palms.

Day two is the best walk on Great Barrier and one of the best in the Auckland region. It follows Palmers Track through the jagged spires and rata-covered cliffs of Windy Canyon to the 627 metre summit of Mt Hobson and 360 degree views of the island. From the summit the track descends over a remarkable series of 960 steps and boardwalks to the remains of the most elevated kauri timber dam built on the island. Further on is one of the best-preserved and largest timber dams left in New Zealand; a century-old testament to the ingenuity of loggers in getting felled timber out of the rugged hinterland. These may be public

North Island robins (toutouwai) (top left), taken from the Hauraki Gulf wildlife sanctuary Tiritiri Matangi, were released on the Kotuku Peninsula in 2005 in a project organised by the Bouzaids. Of the 27 birds released, five pairs have remained on the peninsula and successfully bred while the others have moved further afield. Black petrel (bottom right), Pacific gecko (top right) and brown teal (pateke) are among the other rare species to make a home at Glenfern.

tracks but there is a treat in store for Bouzaid's guests who follow the Kaiaraara Stream to Bush's Beach. Waiting there for them are refreshments and Bouzaid's yacht, *Rainbow V*, last of a noble line and return transport to Fitzroy House wharf and Seaview Cottage.

The third day is another classic Barrier tramp, a five- to six-hour walk, beginning with a visit to the Kaitoke Hot Springs and a soak for those who want it. From the springs the track leads through native bush and over 280 metre Mt Maungapiko until it reaches the coast at Kiwiriki Bay, where *Rainbow V* is again waiting with afternoon tea and a ride back to Fitzroy House. If time allows the group are taken to see the 'Barrier Gold' kanuka oil products made by Sven Stellin on the shore of Wairahi Bay. On the final day the group walk the Waterfall Track loop, another short bush walk at Port Fitzroy, leaving time to make connections for return transport to Auckland—although it is possible to stay longer and take in other activities, such as sea-kayaking.

As well as the four-day walks programme, Bouzaid also runs guided walks through Glenfern Sanctuary with all takings going to the Glenfern Sanctuary Charitable Trust.

The suspension bridge at Glenfern Sanctuary (top) leads into the crown of a kauri tree that has commanding views of the bush-clad valley. (Below) Walkers cool off with a swim to the 'ferry' back to Fitzroy harbour. (Previous page) Fitzroy Harbour, with Little Barrier Island in the distance, pictured at sunset from the summit of Mt Hobson.

Time Four days, three nights
Length Variable
Type Native bush, coastal
Start/finish Fitzroy House
Catering No
Pack carry Not required
Special features Bird life and bush
Party number Six
Accommodation Fully featured cottage
Bedding Supplied
Season 1 September to 31 May
Further information www.fitzroyhouse.co.nz

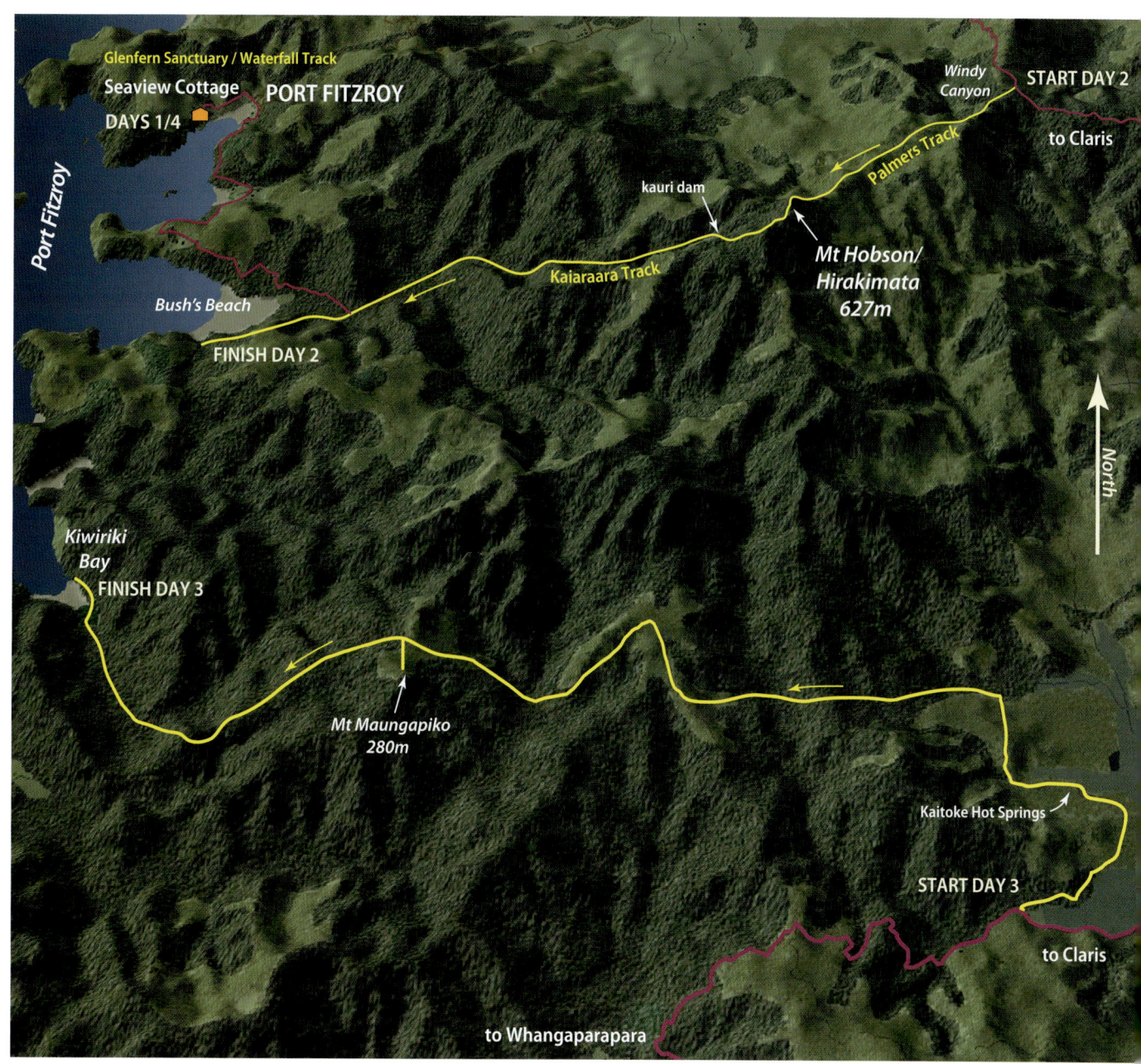

GLENFERN SANCTUARY WALKS, GREAT BARRIER ISLAND

ROAMING IN THE GLOAMING
DUNDLE HILL WALK, WAITOMO, KING COUNTRY

Waitomo farmers Chris and Louise Kay face an unusual stock problem; sometimes one of their sheep or cattle will just disappear, swallowed up by the earth. In the karst limestone country of the South Waikato a tomo (hole) may remain hidden for years until an unfortunate animal happens to step onto a thin covering of earth or scrub and fall down the hole drilled into the limestone by an ancient watercourse.

Even Pooh Bear could not devise a more cunning Heffalump trap. Known tomos are fenced off, but one year 27 cattle fell into previously unknown tomos on the Kay's Tumu Tumu farm. 'Out of 1000 cattle we might lose 1 per cent,' says Chris Kay. 'It's an ongoing problem; I lost a heifer down a 10 metre tomo just the other day.' Fortunately most animals survive the Heffalump traps without injury—much to the delight of Waitomo's professional caving guides, says Chris. 'If you tell them that rescuing an animal can't be done, it becomes a challenge and they will go to extraordinary lengths with ropes and belay systems to get it out.'

Stock-swallowing holes in the ground aside, the 1387 hectare farm—327 hectares of it leasehold pasture—which Kay's parents moved onto when he was three years old, is an exciting property, running 3200 Perendale ewes and ewe hoggets and 1000 cattle. Some 202 hectares of the farm are in plantation forestry, 285 hectares in native bush and 70 hectares in regenerating bush. But of most significance,

Kay's Cabin—a giant hay barn with bunks for 32 walkers and views as far as Mt Ruapehu.

perhaps, is that some 5 kilometres of the upper reaches of the Waitomo Stream run along the farm boundary, meaning the paddocks of Tumu Tumu are a major contributor to the watercourse on which much of the region's famous tourist caving systems depend.

This is a wet area—the Kays' farm can get up to 254 centimetres of rain a year—and it is hilly, rising to almost 350 metres. That means that a lot of water is running off Waitomo farms like Tumu Tumu. In the days when farmers were given subsidies to encourage them to graze steep land, it meant that a lot of soil was slipping into streams and rapidly silting up Waitomo's caves with mud. In the 1970s it was estimated that the famous glow-worm grotto faced the prospect of being drowned in sediment within 50 years. 'Our farming practice was turning the caves into a muddy mess,' admits Chris Kay.

Before it was too late, local farmers, in conjunction with the tourist operators, the Queen Elizabeth II Trust, the Department of Conservation, the Waitomo District Council and Environment Waikato, formed the Waitomo Catchment Trust Board. In 1992 it began a comprehensive programme

22   DUNDLE HILL WALK, WAITOMO, KING COUNTRY

of retiring marginal land and fencing off waterways. More than a million dollars has been spent on fencing off and retiring native bush from grazing, building silt dams, and eradicating goats and possums. The improvement in water quality has been dramatic and the programme is a benchmark studied by other areas in New Zealand with similar problems.

The Kays entered into the land-care programme with such enthusiasm that they won two environmental awards for their efforts. The couple had an added incentive—the 650 metre-long Tumu Tumu cave runs under the farm and is used as a commercial black-water rafting cave, visited by about 9000 people a year. The farm's leasehold land also contains two other popular tourist caves, Haggas Honking Holes and St Benedict's Caverns, run by Waitomo Adventures. And near the homestead is the 30 metre-high Tumu Tumu Rock that Maori legend says a princess jumped off when her men did not fight, and a rare Maori fortress built with dry-stone walls.

The increasing focus on the history and sustainable environment of their farm, along with the daily arrival of young adventurers to Tumu Tumu Toobing, got Chris and Louise Kay thinking about how else they might diversify into tourism and share their environment with others. 'We started to wonder what else we could do in Waitomo,' says Chris. 'Louise and I are both into walking so that interested us. And the farm is dominated by this ice cream-shaped hill and we thought it would be neat to do something up there.'

The idea soon became reality. A large lodge based on a four-bay hay barn—'we thought we'd only get one crack at it so we decided to go big,' says Chris—was built on top of the 'ice cream', Dundle Hill, and the private walk was ready for its first walkers at the end of 2002. The walk

Kay's Cabin (bottom left and right) is huge and surrounded by bush (above) but a wood-burning fire keeps it warm and cosy with the snug ambience of a limestone cave (right). The region, renowned for its glow-worm caves, is riddled with caves and tomos carved through the ancient seabed limestone. Three popular tourist caves are under the Kays' farm.

24 DUNDLE HILL WALK, WAITOMO, KING COUNTRY

was planned to fit with Waitomo's tourist attractions and so starts and finishes at the village, opposite the Waitomo Museum of Caves.

The first day of 14 kilometres takes five to seven hours. It begins on the Waitomo Walkway, a one-and-a-half hour DOC walk past sculptured rocks and fluted limestone outcrops to the popular Ruakuri Bush Scenic Reserve. Dundle Hill walkers soon leave the reserve to follow their own trail across pasture and native bush on Tumu Tumu farm, before climbing through a plantation forest to the 325 metre top of Dundle Hill and the lodge. The site was naturally clear and once a haven for wild pigs to rest in the sun. From the lodge deck there are commanding views to Mt Ruapehu, Mt Pirongia, Marokopa Beach and Maungatautari Mountain. In the evening the banks of a bench-cut track just below the lodge shimmer with glow-worms. The spacious lodge interior is lined with unpainted and fragrant macrocarpa and Lawson's cypress.

Day two of 13 kilometres is easier, taking four to five hours. Not far from the start a side track leads to the entrance of Olsens Wet Cave, birthplace of the Waitomo Stream and home to some huge cave wetas. The cave, first explored in the early 1950s, is 608 metres long and more than 19 metres wide, its roof a panoply of glow-worms. The trail then follows the Waitomo Stream downhill past Cowan's Corner, a small patch of bush where eels lurk in the stream waiting for food scraps, before reaching the top of the Ruakuri Reserve and the Waitomo Waterfall.

Much of this 114 hectares of native bush was first protected in 1905 and contains many large rimu and kahikatea, classic limestone outcrops, caves, tunnels, gorges and cantilevered walkways high above the rushing water. The Dundle Hill track zig zags through the bush—DOC is planning to upgrade the track to the falls—before joining a loop track past the Ruakuri natural tunnel, Ruakuri Cave and adjacent Aranui cave, rejoining the Waitomo Walkway to return to

The Waitomo Stream lies at the heart of much of the Waitomo cave system and borders long stretches of the Dundle Hill Walk.

the Waitomo village. 'People usually stay in Waitomo before or after the walk and get into the atmosphere of the place,' says Chris Kay.

A recent addition is the HuHu complex, at the northern end of the village where you'll find a gift store, cafe and ticket kiosk.

The Kays have made a point of putting information signs at strategic locations along the trail.

'We want people doing this walk to learn about how the catchment works,' says Chris. The ultimate understanding might be to fall down a tomo but if they stick to the track, Dundle Hill walkers have no fear of that.

Time Two days, one night
Length 27 kilometres
Type Farm, native bush, plantation forest, DOC reserve
Start/finish Waitomo village
Catering On request
Pack carry Yes
Special features Caving option, glow-worms
Party number Up to 32
Accommodation Purpose built lodge, showers, and fully-equipped kitchen with gas hob
Bedding No
Season October to May
Further information www.waitomowalk.com

Water is as much a part of the Waitomo region as its caves. Over aeons water slowly dissolves limestone that was once on the seabed, to create narrow fissures (right), caves and tomos. In the early morning mist lies over the sodden pasture (left) as the land begins to heat up.

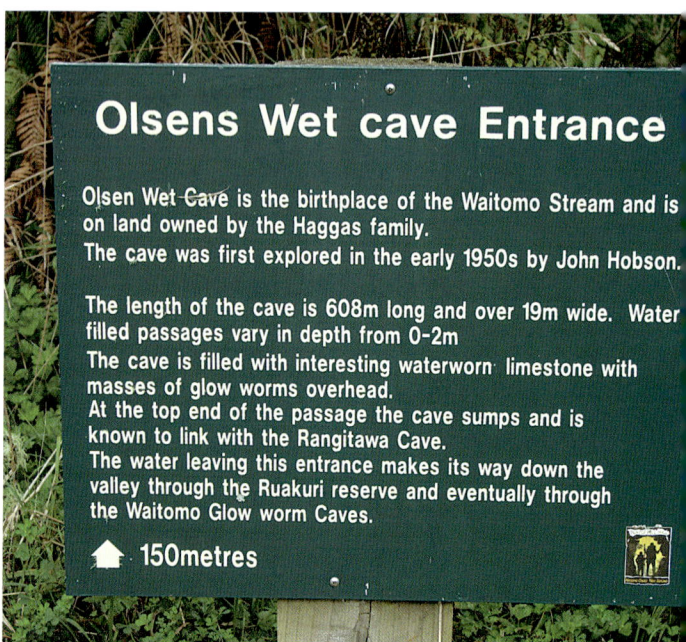

28 DUNDLE HILL WALK, WAITOMO, KING COUNTRY

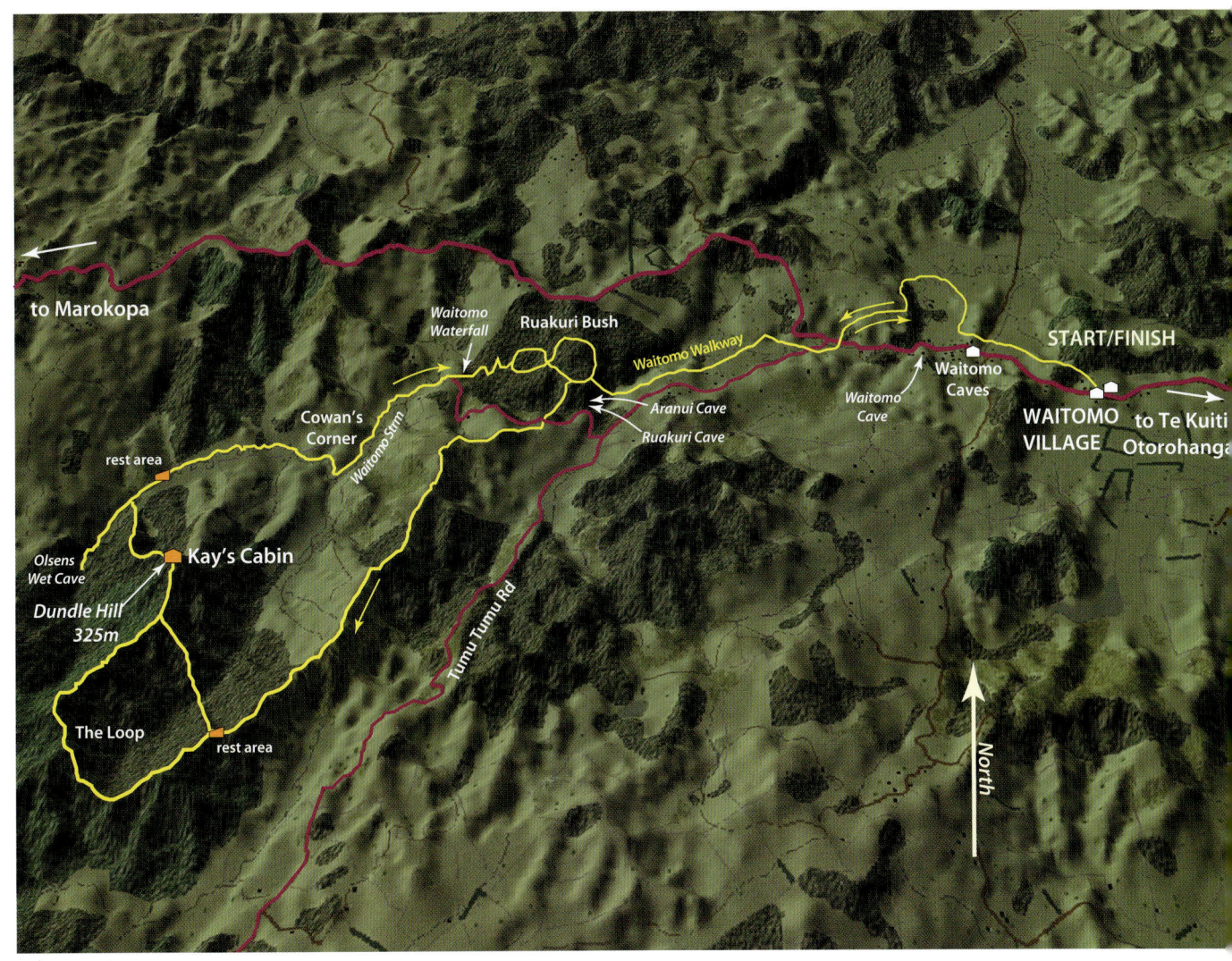

Tumu Tumu Rock (top left) rises 30 metres above peaceful pasture but was once the scene of a dramatic protest. According to Maori legend a princess jumped from the top when her men would not fight. Nearby is a rare Maori fortress built with dry-stone walls. Glow-worms and cave wetas (bottom left) are creatures of the dark.

DUNDLE HILL WALK, WAITOMO, KING COUNTRY

LUXURY, SHEER LUXURY
WALK GISBORNE, GISBORNE

What would the Scouts or Girls Brigaders of Gisborne think of the camp menu? Where are the sausages and lumpy porridge? What on earth is this 'Moroccan lamb tagine, spiced casserole with fruit, nuts and couscous, served with a fresh garden salad'? It may not sound like tramping food, but it is what happens when a dedicated foodie sets up a walking track on the family farm and gives it the focus 'taste the experience.'

Penny Hoogerbrug grew up on a sheep and cattle station at Ruatoria until she moved to Auckland to follow a career in nursing. In 1985, when her father, Colin Williams, moved his Kaharau Angus Stud to the 1200 hectare Rimunui Station on the northern outskirts of Gisborne, Penny and her husband, Pete, returned to run a 20 hectare apple and kiwifruit orchard that was on Karakaroa Farm, Rimunui's original homestead block from the days when the station was part of the much larger Rimuroa Station. Twenty-two years later, with returns falling, the vines and fruit trees came out, the land was restored to farmland, and Pete became a produce marketing executive in Gisborne.

So what was an energetic countrywoman, with her family almost grown up and time suddenly on her hands, to do? Well, there were horses to ride, a magnificent garden to care for, a woodworking course, regular tramping trips with friends, particularly on the private walks circuit—and the inspiration of the Whana walk run by an old boarding-school mate, Clair MacIntyre. Oh, and one other thing. Down in the back paddock there was the old Girls Brigade hut, built in the 1950s for the Scouts and Girls Brigade of Gisborne, more recently used by a few school groups and to accommodate apple picking gangs, and now surplus to requirements. Put all that together with a large dollop of Penny Hoogerbrug's enthusiasm, and the support and DIY skills of husband, Pete, and you get Walk Gisborne, a private trek with its own distinctive flavour.

The first step was to get the support of neighbours, Richard and Robyn Busby, who have farmed the adjoining 576 hectare Makorori Station since 1987. The Busbys' coastal property drops down to the spectacular Makorori beach, north of Gisborne, and delivers Walk Gisborne trekkers quite stunning views as far as the Mahia Peninsula. Next step was a major makeover for the old Girls Brigade hut. Photographs tell the quite amazing transformation that the Hoogerbrugs have wrought on the corrugated-iron shed. The boys and girls who used to doss down on the floor for a weekend camp in the country would barely recognise their old camp site. The renovation has been cleverly done so that, for instance, the old roof with stencilling on the

An iconic New Zealand scene remains common in rural Gisborne, where horses are still used by shepherds and stockmen.

32 WALK GISBORNE, GISBORNE

corrugated iron has been retained as an interior lining to maintain the character.

Many of the furnishings, such as the large diningroom table, were built by Penny from macrocarpa sourced from further up the coast. A nice touch is a Girls Brigade wooden camp gear box beside each bed, and Penny has added something not found on other private walks—each bunk has a monogrammed fleece blanket, and there is a full linen service if you want. Fresh towels are provided daily at a small cost. The second accommodation building, the old shearers' quarters on Rimunui Station, has also been renovated with style. Both lodges have a fully equipped kitchen, and if you are a tramping Grinch you might take your boring de-hy along for a typical DOC-hut, totally forgettable meal.

But anyone with a touch of class, not to mention adventure, will take advantage of the arrangement between Walk Gisborne and top Gisborne chef, Darryn Clyne, and his Champagne Catering Company and enjoy magnificent food and wine delivered to the lodges each night. Imagine the following: kumara-and-orange-stuffed chicken breast with a zesty cinnamon spiced baste, served with creamy sliced potato galette, roast vegetables and vegetable medley followed by individual meringue nests with chocolate top, berry compote and cream. Beats adding water to a packet any day. If you want, imaginative nibble platters can be waiting for you each day, with a range of local cheese, spreads and dried fruits, and Gisborne wines.

But in between all this pampering there is some walking to do—beside streams, over open pasture, on bulldozed farm tracks, trails cut through pockets of native bush, and down to the sea. The trek includes many points of interest—a pa site, kumara pits and the unusual mud volcanoes—all signposted and marked on a map each walker is given. Penny already knew the station well, but

The Gisborne region is renowned for its surf beaches, sunshine, fine cuisine and Chardonnay—features that are all included in the Walk Gisborne package. Girls Brigade and Scouting memorabilia have been retained to decorate the former Girls Brigade cabin (middle and bottom). Bentonitic mud (left) bubbles with escaping methane gas.

WALK GISBORNE, GISBORNE   33

on walking and riding over it extensively to plot the walk, she managed to walk in some lovely patches of bush that she hadn't previously been in.

Day one, which is 12 kilometres and about five hours long, starts from the Girls Brigade hut and crosses the Waimata River, through native bush, and uphill to The Peak. At 323 metres, The Peak gives extensive views to the Mahia Peninsula, Young Nicks Head and north to Mt Hikurangi. Overnight is at the shearers' quarters where, if you wish, you can indulge in something special after your day's walk—lie back in a tastefully furnished room and enjoy a massage at the hands of a qualified Gisborne masseuse. Sheer bliss.

That should set you up nicely to head off on day two, a walk to the coast of up to 16.5 kilometres and six and a half hours. There are two shorter alternatives but the full walk includes a bush remnant dominated by a giant puriri tree, a trig station at 239 metres with coastal views to die for, historic Maori sites, and lunch and a swim on Makorori Beach, before returning on a loop to the shearers' quarters for a second night.

Day three is a fairly moderate 9.5 kilometres and about three and a half hours, back to the Girls Brigade hut, but also including a 210 metre high point with commanding views, and the strange geological phenomenon of mud volcanoes. These patches of bubbling mud are from a seam of bentonitic mud many millions of years old that emits salt water and natural gas, mainly methane. The gas causes the mud to quietly bubble, but there have been large eruptions as well. One in 1908 sent mud 150 metres into the air. Another in 1930 ejected about 150,000 tonnes

Sometimes you don't get the chance to enjoy what is in your own backyard. Walking around the family farm to plot Walk Gisborne allowed Penny Hoogerbrug to tramp through patches of native bush and old puriri trees for the first time.

The shearers' quarters (right) has been tastefully renovated for accommodation on nights one and two. It even contains a massage room. The broad sweep of the coast (pp. 36–37) stretches north beyond Makorori Beach, one of Gisborne's renowned surf beaches, and tantalises walkers.

WALK GISBORNE, GISBORNE 35

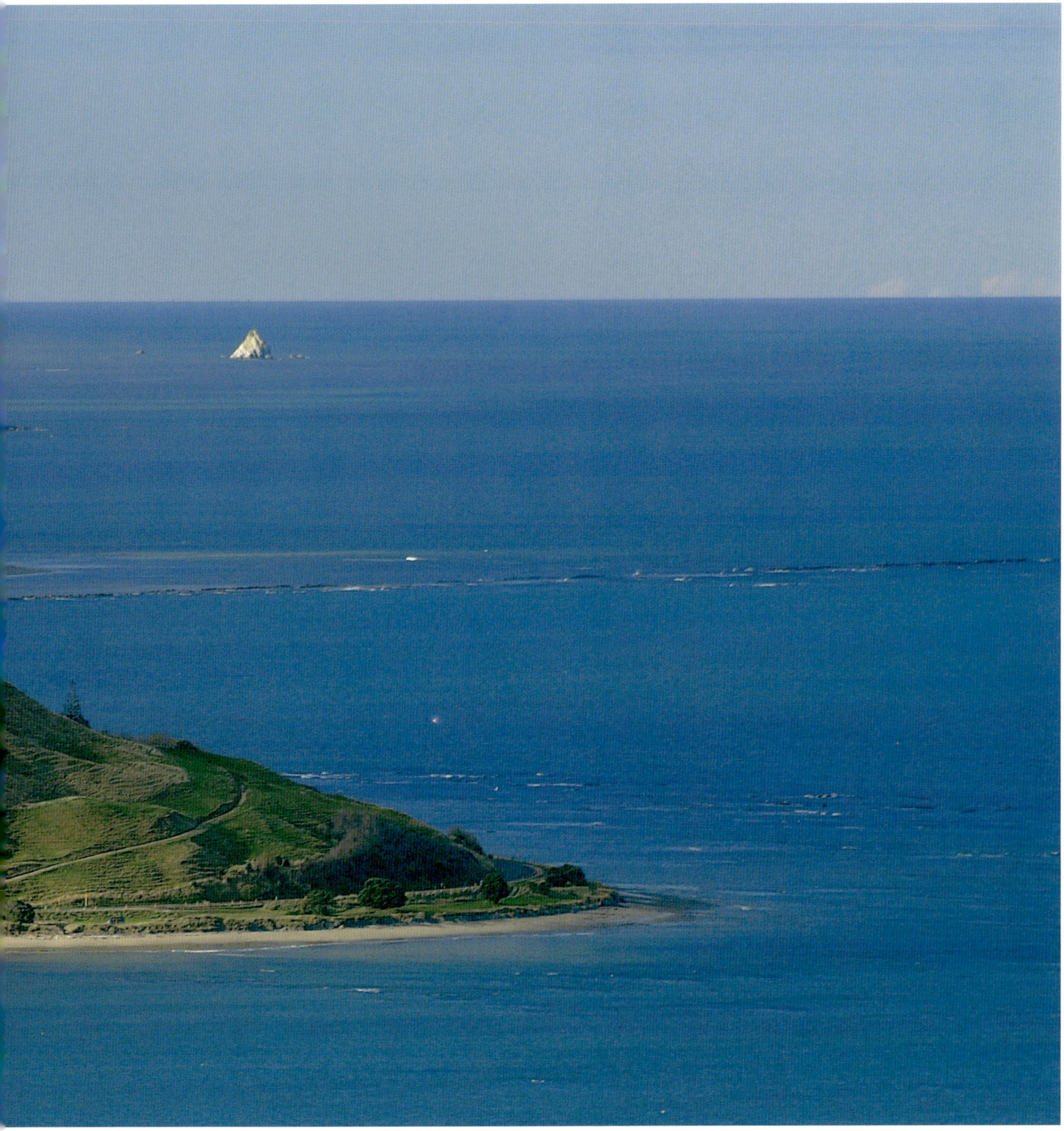

of mud, burying a nearby valley to a depth of 10 metres. It is not all bad news though—the bentonitic mud is used for farm road metalling and to seal leaky drains. The mud is also used as an ingredient in face cream—which after three days of pampered luxury seems the most appropriate way to remember this otherwise ugly patch of bubbling mud.

Time Two or three days/nights
Length 40 kilometres
Type Farm and coastal
Start/finish Girls Brigade Hut, Karakaroa Farm
Catering Yes
Pack carry Yes
Special features Stunning cuisine, massage service
Party number 12
Accommodation Two comfortable and fully equipped lodges
Bedding Available
Season Labour Weekend until 30 April
Further information www.walkgisborne.co.nz

Moderate and sometimes challenging terrain befits a walk where at the end of the day you can pamper yourself with a massage and cuisine prepared by one of Gisborne's top chefs.

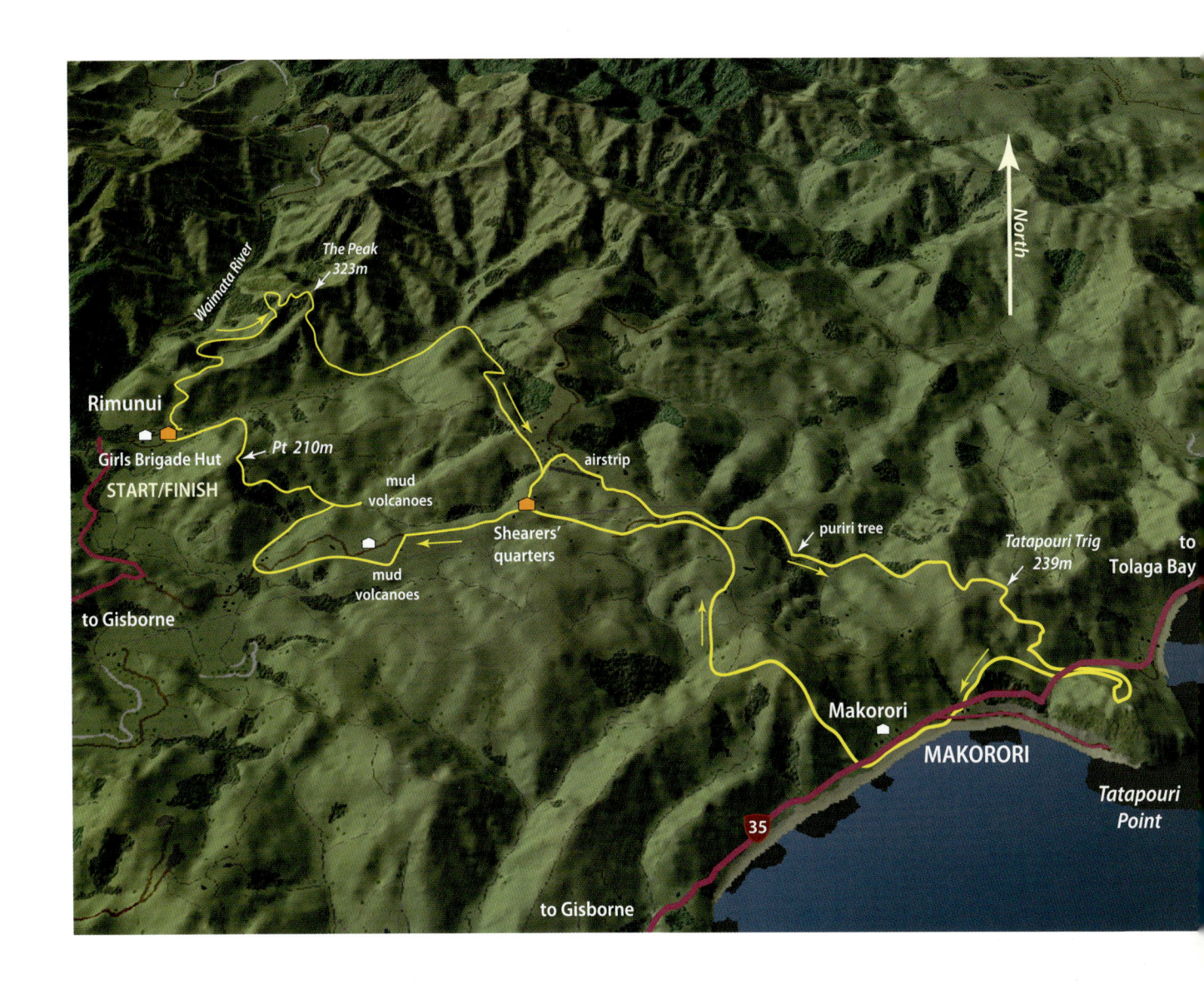

WALK GISBORNE, GISBORNE 39

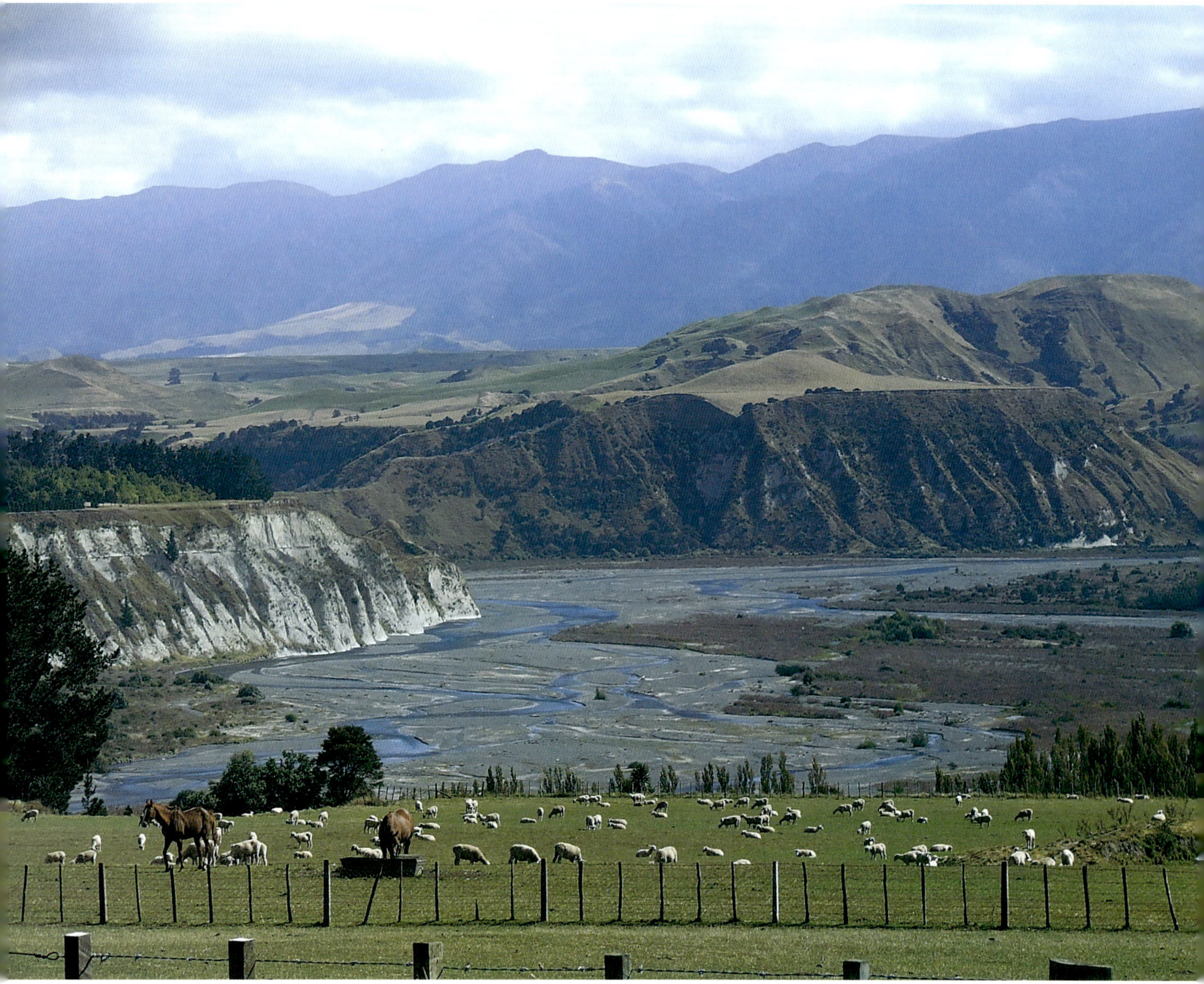

FOOTPRINTS ON A CANVAS
WHANA WALK, HAWKE'S BAY

The broad, alluvial flats of the Ngaruroro River are the backbone of Hawke's Bay's renowned wine industry. Follow the river inland from its mouth between Napier and Hastings, and the Ngaruroro's old river terraces are lined, kilometre after kilometre, with neat rows of grapevines.

The vines follow the broad swathe of the river's path on shingly, free-draining soils whose low fertility assures award-winning wines, almost to the northern Ruahine and southern Kaweka Ranges, from where the river begins its long path to the sea. When the river terraces eventually narrow and disappear, so do the vines. And then, quite suddenly, over a small rise, lies a startling contrast to the rigid rows of grapes—a broad valley of rolling, green hills, tall poplars and lines of stately pine windbreaks. Maori called this delightful valley Whana Whana, in deference to a taniwha being dragged across country to a new watery home at Lake Taupo. The water spirit got this far before it began to 'kick kick' as it tried to break free from its bonds. You can see the outcome of its struggles in the deeply incised and winding course of the upper reaches of the Ngaruroro and the Mangarakau Stream as they flow out of the Kawekas. But elsewhere the Whana Whana Valley is worthy of a painting by Constable.

The Ngaruroro River shows its glacial origins with broad, braided reaches.

Of course, it didn't look anything like that in 1878 when George Beamish stood on the same small rise looking for a mob of horses that had gone AWOL from a farm near Hastings. In 1849 his father, Nathaniel, then a 21-year-old Irishman, had sailed to the infant colony with fatherly directions to 'spy out the land.' Nearly 30 years later young George took similar instructions in search of horses and found a valley, then owned by a Maori princess, that made sufficient impression for him to start a Beamish dynasty at Whana Whana that exists to this day. The Beamish family initially farmed about 7530 hectares, but in 1910 George split the farm among his three sons. They shared a common woolshed where the road ended just before climbing up to the rise overlooking the valley.

Son Noel farmed the Awapai block. His son, Ralph, built a road down into the valley and Awapai's own woolshed and shearers' quarters—from where, today, Ralph's daughter, Clair MacIntyre, and her husband, Peter, run the Whana Walk. There is even a spa at the roomy and much modernised workers' bunkhouse, as well as a full kitchen. But why bother cooking when you can get full catering, prepared and delivered by Clair. Breakfast and lunch can also be provided.

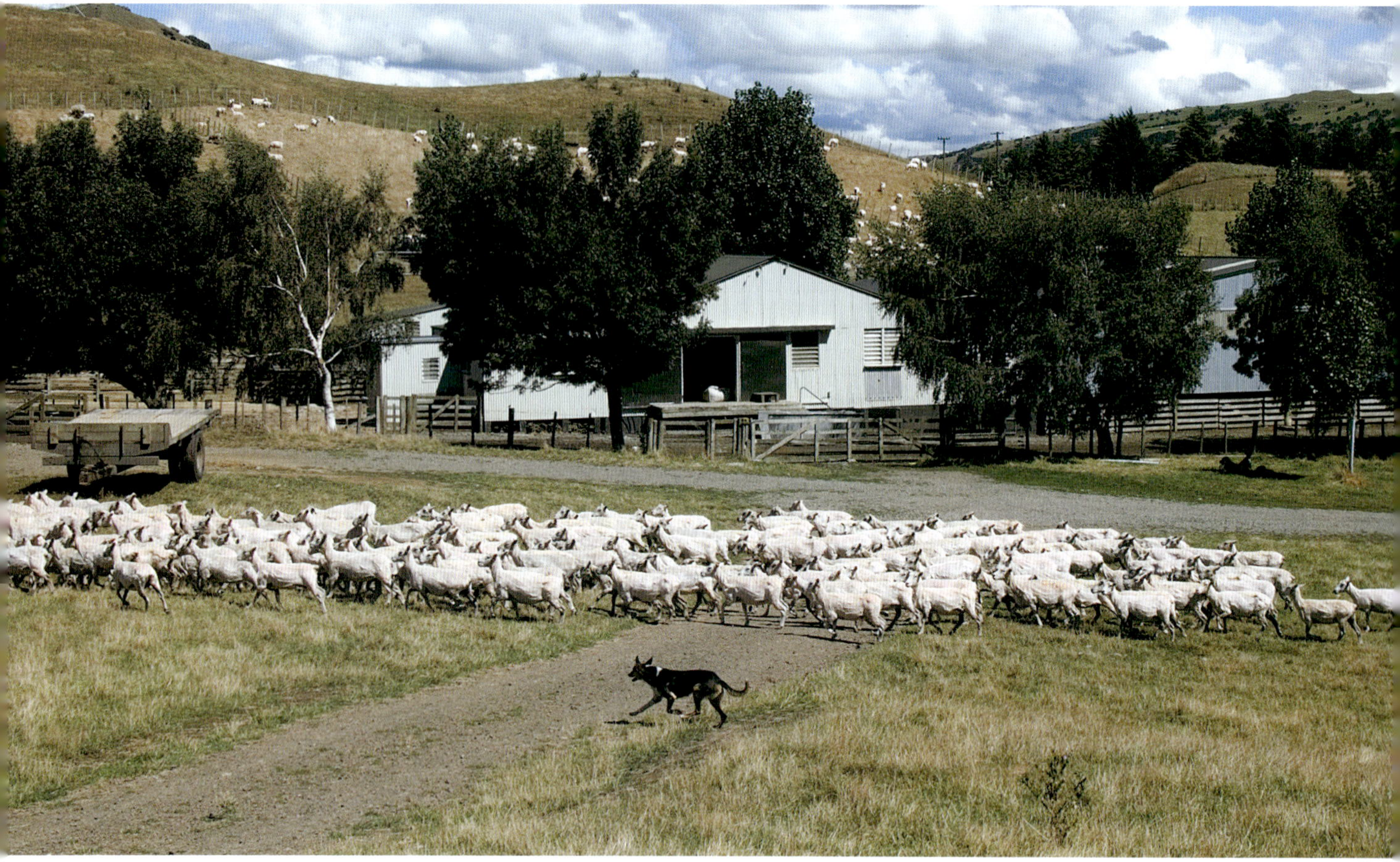

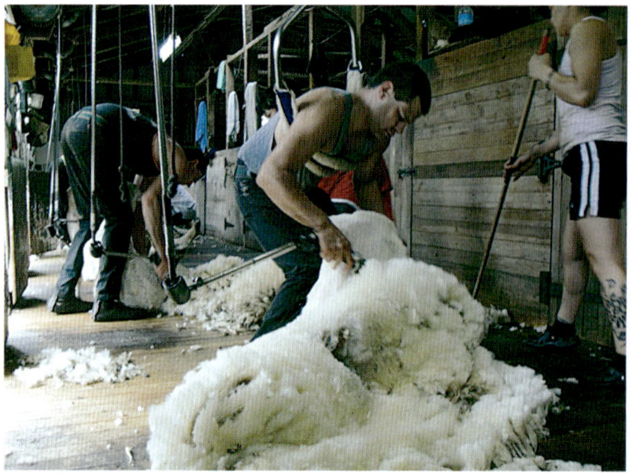

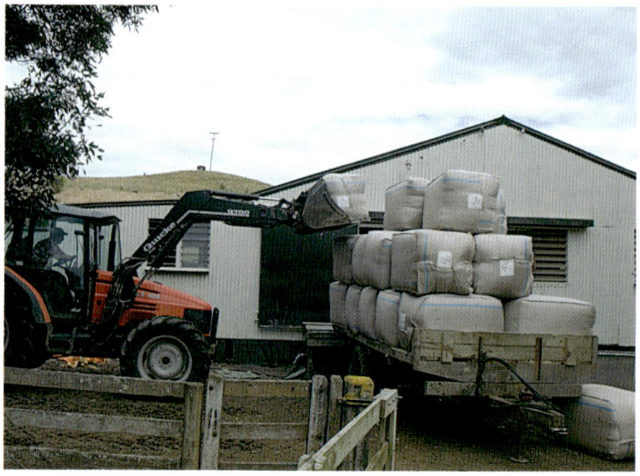

At the end of the walking season the MacIntyres move between Clair's grandparents' old house and a home in Wellington, where Peter is a top executive in the electricity industry, although if you stop at The Old House on your way into Awapai you will wonder how the family can ever bear to leave its elderly trees, cottage gardens, and the braying of a donkey in an adjoining paddock.

The Whana Walk consists of three distinct circuits, with colour-coded markers—blue, orange and red—that all start and finish at the accommodation. The blue circuit has three options of varying length, from a few hours to seven hours. The long track leads down to the places where the taniwha did his kicking thing and, while any of the options on the blue circuit is officially the track for the first day's walk, it may well be best to leave the long option until the end. By then you have got into the spirit of things and are not fazed by following the bush-clad Mangarakau Gorge and Omahaki Stream until it meets with the Ngaruroro River.

Here you can swim or try your luck at trout fishing before tackling the steep climb out. The short alternative exits at the Mangarakau Stream and returns over pasture to the Awapai quarters. A medium alternative, taking from five and a half to six and a half hours, climbs onto a 563-metre ridge summit south of the Mangarakau Gorge. It is an excellent spot for lunch with views of the massive escarpments of the Ngaruroro Gorge and, weather permitting, across Hawke Bay to Cape Kidnappers.

The day two walk is colour-coded orange and focuses on one of three bush reserves that Ralph Beamish covenanted to the Queen Elizabeth II Trust in 1994. As well as fencing the land off from stock, Ralph and his son, Simon, who now farms Awapai, started an ongoing tree-planting and

(Right) Three bush reserves covenanted to the Queen Elizabeth II Trust are being extensively re-planted with native species. The reserves are fenced off from stock but elsewhere this is very much a working farm.

(Left) The accommodation is in the old Awapai shearers' quarters. If you are lucky your stay will coincide with a shearing gang working in the shearing shed nearby.

pest-eradication programme. A feature of Little Bush, as the reserve is known on the farm, is an enormous kahikatea, many hundreds of years old. From here, the trail climbs a high ridge called Pukehau, which gives great views into the Kawekas, until entering Henry's Bush, another Queen Elizabeth II covenant with a more extensive variety of native trees than Little Bush and an even larger kahikatea. Bird life is prolific, especially kereru.

But the highlight of this circuit, perhaps, is to climb a ridge to the skyline. A fence here marks the boundary of the Beamish property—an enormous split totara strainer post dates back to the original nineteenth-century boundary fence—but a stile lets you go just a few metres further to a trig at 679 metres. The 360 degree view is spectacular—into the Kaweka Ranges, sometimes as far as Mt Ruapehu, and towards the Gentle Annie (the Napier–Taihape road), Napier, Hastings, and south to the Ruahines.

The route back to the Awapai quarters first passes through a windswept plateau of ash-type soil that is known in Beamish circles as 'No Man's Land.' As a girl, Clair, her

The longest walk leads down the Omahaki Stream to the Ngaruroro River. If you are a trout fisher there is an extra reason for choosing the longest trail. On the highest ground there are huge limestone rocks (below) embedded with fossil shells.

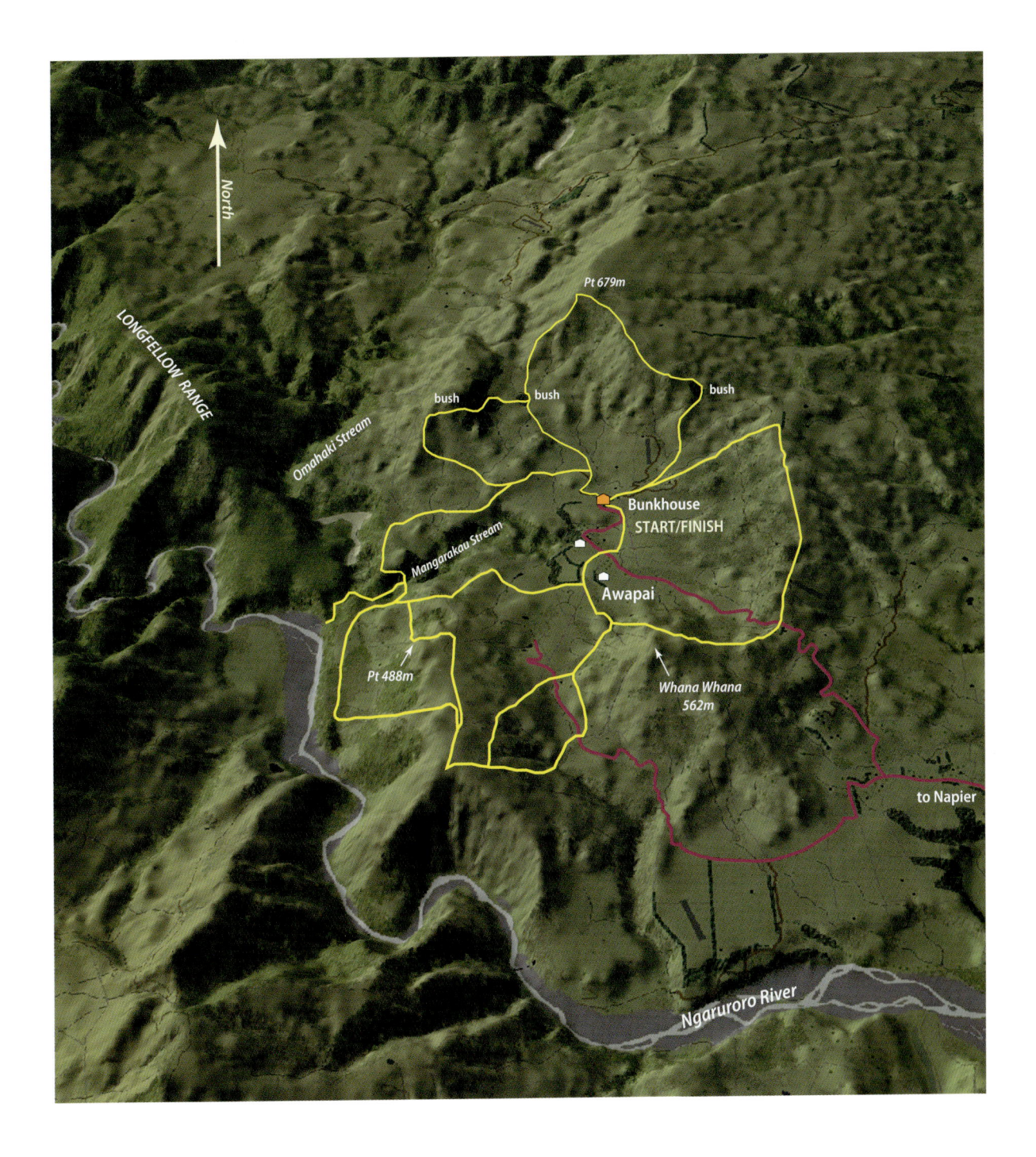

WHANA WALK, HAWKE'S BAY 45

46   WHANA WALK, HAWKE'S BAY

WHANA WALK, HAWKE'S BAY

siblings, cousins and friends, would ride their horses to this spot, once reminiscent of the terrain often seen in John Wayne-era Western movies, and play cowboys and Indians. A pine plantation has since softened the landscape but there is still sufficient atmosphere there for you to envy the country kids who could play their games on real horses instead of imaginary ones. Horses are Clair's first love and she used to compete at top level in three-day eventing competitions. One of her eventing horses was reserve for an Olympic training squad. Peter MacIntyre, who is also from a Hawke's Bay farming family, shares his wife's passion for horses, and the couple regularly ride around the farm and on multi-day horse treks.

The descent from No Man's Land is rich with views of the Whana Whana Valley's rolling pastoral landscape. The trail includes a traverse through one last native bush reserve,

A totara strainer post on the highest point of the Whana walks is the original 19th century boundary marker for the property settled by George Beamish. His great granddaughter, Clair, and her husband Peter MacIntyre (below) run the Whana Walk.

Karamu Bush. The orange circuit also has two shorter options that do not climb to the high point of the track.

The day three track, colour-coded red, takes four to five hours, and is mostly a farm trek over roller-coaster pastureland and through some groves of exotic trees. The view, however, is constantly expansive. The trail also reveals one startling aspect of this land—along a ridge at more than 300 metres above sea level, are huge outcrops of limestone embedded with fossil shells. The sea is now nearly 50 kilometres away but once it swept right across those many hectares of vineyards to lap at the foot of the Ruahine and Kaweka Ranges.

Fossil shells from a primeval sea are found on a ridge (above) far from the ocean. (Pp. 46–47) The Ngaruroro follows the path of an ancient glacier.

Time One to four nights and days
Length Up to 36 kilometres
Type Farm and bush
Start/finish Awapai Quarters, Whana Whana Road
Catering On demand
Pack carry Not required
Special features Trout fishing
Party number Up to 14
Accommodation Fully self-contained lodge with seven double bedrooms
Bedding Not supplied
Season Labour weekend to 30 April
Further information whanawalkhawkesbay@xtra.co.nz

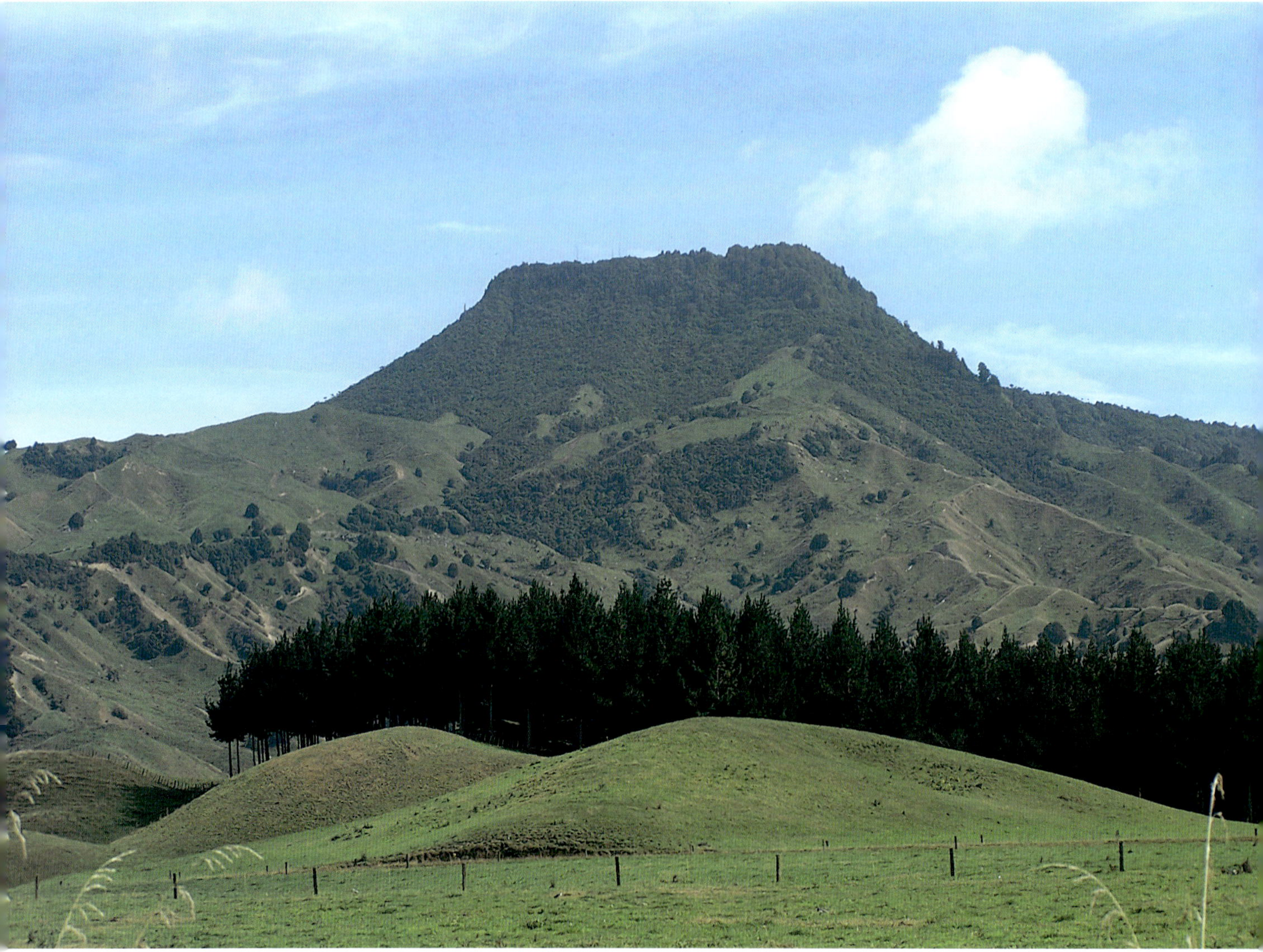

THE ANSWER LIES IN THE SOIL
WALK WESTRIDGE, ONGARUE, NEAR TAUMARUNUI

By rights there shouldn't be a decent native tree left standing in the King Country. For the first half of the twentieth century the vast indigenous forests in the centre of the North Island were mercilessly logged, their rimu giants milled to frame houses, the matai used for flooring, and the totara to build bridges and lay beneath steel railway lines.

The Maori King Tawhiao kept the forests of the Rohe Potae safe for a while, but the main trunk railway snaking south could not be contained at the border forever. Rewi Maniapoto, who led the opposition to the British, dug the first sods for the line to enter the King Country in 1885; by 1901 it had reached Ongarue and nearby Taumarunui 'on the Main Trunk Line,' where generations of train travellers would later stop to grab a pie and a cup of tea.

The magnificent podocarp forests of the Mangakahu Valley near Ongarue, long considered by Maori as a 'bountiful food basket,' were doomed. Within a couple of years a sawmilling company, Ellis and Burnand, second in size only to the giant Kauri Timber Company, began to fell the trees and build 80 kilometres of bush tramway, with ingenious feats of engineering, including tall, curving viaducts of timber, to get the logs to their sawmill at Ongarue on the main rail line.

From 5210 hectares of bush near Ongarue that had grown unmolested for centuries on volcanic ash blown from the enormous Taupo eruption of AD181, the timber

Mt Hikurangi (770 metres) which dominates the Ongarue skyline, is revered by Ngati Maniapoto.

men milled tens of millions of metres of native timber—enough to build nearly 11,500 complete timber homes. In their wake came a hardy bunch of settlers to clear the rest of the bush and turn the pumice hills into farms. Among them, in 1919, was Percy Beard. His granddaughter would marry the boy next door, Alex Fraser, and their son, Mason, and his wife, Sue, would turn the clock back more than a century to create a bush and farmland walk that defies the land's recent history.

Walk Westridge, looping through 1375 hectares of the old Beard and Fraser properties—Mason's brother Ewen Fraser farms another portion of the original farms—encompasses pasture, ignimbrite rock formations, important Maori cultural sites and a surprising amount of lush forest that over 50 years has made a dramatic recovery from the ravages of axe and saw. The farm is also bordered on three sides by the Pureora Forest Park, which is a bit like having a fishing spot on the boundary of a marine reserve. The extensive bush remnants on Westridge Farm have benefited enormously from possum, rat and stoat poisoning which was a TB pest programme undertaken by Horizon's Regional Council on behalf of the Animal Health Board, and are now abundant with birdlife such as kereru—Mason has seen 60 to 70 of

52 WALK WESTRIDGE, ONGARUE, NEAR TAUMARUNUI

the native pigeons in one flock—tui, bellbirds, cuckoos and whiteheads.

Sue Fraser is a keen tramper and, after walking tracks such as the Milford, Hump Ridge and Tora, decided there were walks in her own backyard that were just as good. A walking business was a chance to create a small enterprise of her own and to meet people. Fortuitously, an adjoining property that had been bought came with a small cottage that makes an ideal base for walkers and is close enough to allow Sue to cater for them—a service she particularly enjoys providing. Ironically, the loggers left a legacy in the bush that would also be of benefit to walkers. The narrow tramlines benched around the hills so the bush lokeys—small steam locomotives—could haul the log trains out of the bush to the voracious Ongarue mill make excellent walking paths.

The loggers left the Mangakahu Valley in 1932 and, in the intervening years, the 500 hectares of native bush on Westridge that stock are fenced out of have regenerated spectacularly.

The first day's walk is a 15 kilometre loop through the bush that takes about six hours and mostly follows the easy contours taken by the old bush tramway. The forest is predominantly tall and straight tawa, with trees up to 800 years old. Hidden in the undergrowth are stumps of rimu and totara, but there are some large trees the loggers left intact, perhaps because they were used as anchor trees for the rope haulers. One enormous totara is 1800 years old and was probably just too big for the loggers to handle. There are a couple of small huts in the bush that were most recently used by possum trappers, with one now serving as a place for walkers to stop for a breather and a brew up. The Frasers plan to build a lodge somewhere in the bush so that walkers can spend a night in the forest, looking down on the valley below, with Mt Hikurangi (770 metres),

Possum control on the adjoining Pureora Forest Park ensures the rata trees (right) at Westridge flower in profusion. In the bush, where the undergrowth is lush with a wide variety of ferns (top right), a totara estimated to be 1800 years old (bottom left) somehow survived the logging era. One that didn't was left behind as a handy bridge.

54 WALK WESTRIDGE, ONGARUE, NEAR TAUMARUNUI

WALK WESTRIDGE, ONGARUE, NEAR TAUMARUNUI

historically and spiritually connected to Ngati Maniapoto, towering in the distance.

In the 1980s Mason Fraser trapped possums for cash, but the poisoning programme that has largely got rid of them is the best thing to have happened, he says. The bush is now healthy with fresh growth no longer stripped off, and the rata again flower profusely. The farm also used to lose up to 60 animals a year to tuberculosis, but it has been clear for the last 12 years.

Day two is a loop of around 11 kilometres, taking about six hours and again on the easy contours of the old tramway, mostly through the 850 hectares of pasture on Westridge. The tramway used to pass close to Mason's home, previously his grandparents' house, a transport convenience that Mason's grandfather often made use of to get stock or supplies to and from the Ongarue station.

The story is told of Grandfather Beard watching five years of wool clip that he had been storing until the market improved disappearing down the line at the insistence of his bank manager. Just a few months later the wool price trebled. The walk provides extensive views across pasture and valleys of bush as far as Mt Taranaki and north to Pirongia, with the bush-covered ranges of Pureora Forest Park providing a backdrop. A feature of the second day's walk is several ignimbrite rock formations that overlook the farm like castle battlements.

Ongarue is on the border of three major Maori tribal territories, Ngati Maniapoto, Ngati Haua and Ngati Tuwharetoa. The Mangakahu Valley was at the crossroads of Maori trails north and south and through to Taupo, and the famous fighting pa of Otutewehi lies close to Westridge.

The farm carries 3800 Romney-cross ewes and 350 cows,

A lookout during the Westridge walks (top right) reveals Mt Hikurangi and in the far distance the snow-capped peak of Mt Taranaki. A small farm cottage (bottom right) is a comfortable base for Westridge walkers. A ramble beside the Mangakahu Stream (top left) makes a nice conclusion to Walk Westridge. Forest clearance for farming leaves some unusual relics (bottom left) that fire and rain have not managed to destroy. (Pp. 54–55) Bush soon grows back on areas fenced off from stock.

WALK WESTRIDGE, ONGARUE, NEAR TAUMARUNUI 57

as well as deer, and is managed on 'biological' principles, a farming system that lies somewhere between organic and conventional. 'I got sick of looking at crook stock,' explains Mason. His concerns led him to the biological system, which means he uses drenches and dips on his stock as needs demand without any organic farming prohibitions but at the same time tries to work with nature as much as is possible. The basic tenet is that the answer to healthy stock lies in the soil. Just as the human stomach contains bacteria and microbes to break down food into elements the body can easily absorb, so does the soil; it is the pasture's stomach, says Mason. Grass may absorb straight nitrogen, he says, but the grass will be healthier for stock if the nutrients, such as nitrogen, have first been 'digested' by bacteria and fungi in the soil. To ensure it is, the pasture on Westridge is dosed with mostly natural fertiliser laced with special microbes that previously were deficient in the soil.

Before leaving Westridge there is the opportunity for an extra, and interesting, short walk along an old Maori walking track through tanekaha trees to a private edge of the Mangakahu River, and eventually to a tributary stream that flows through a natural rock tunnel.

Before you leave, make sure you've had a chance to see the unusual beautiful blue sky mushrooms (*Entoloma hochstetteri*) (p.52), named after Austrian geologist Hochstetter who visited the Ongarue marae in 1859.

Time Two or three night option
Length 26 kilometres
Type Native bush, farmland
Start/finish Westridge Farm, Ongarue, Taumarunui
Catering On request
Pack carry Not required
Special features Timber milling history, sky blue mushrooms
Party number Eight
Accommodation Modern cottage, full-serviced kitchen
Bedding Not provided
Season Labour Weekend to end of May.
Further information www.walkwestridge.co.nz

Deer, sheep and cattle graze the Westridge pasture, which is managed according to radical biological principles aimed at enhancing soil quality. Healthy soil makes for healthy stock.

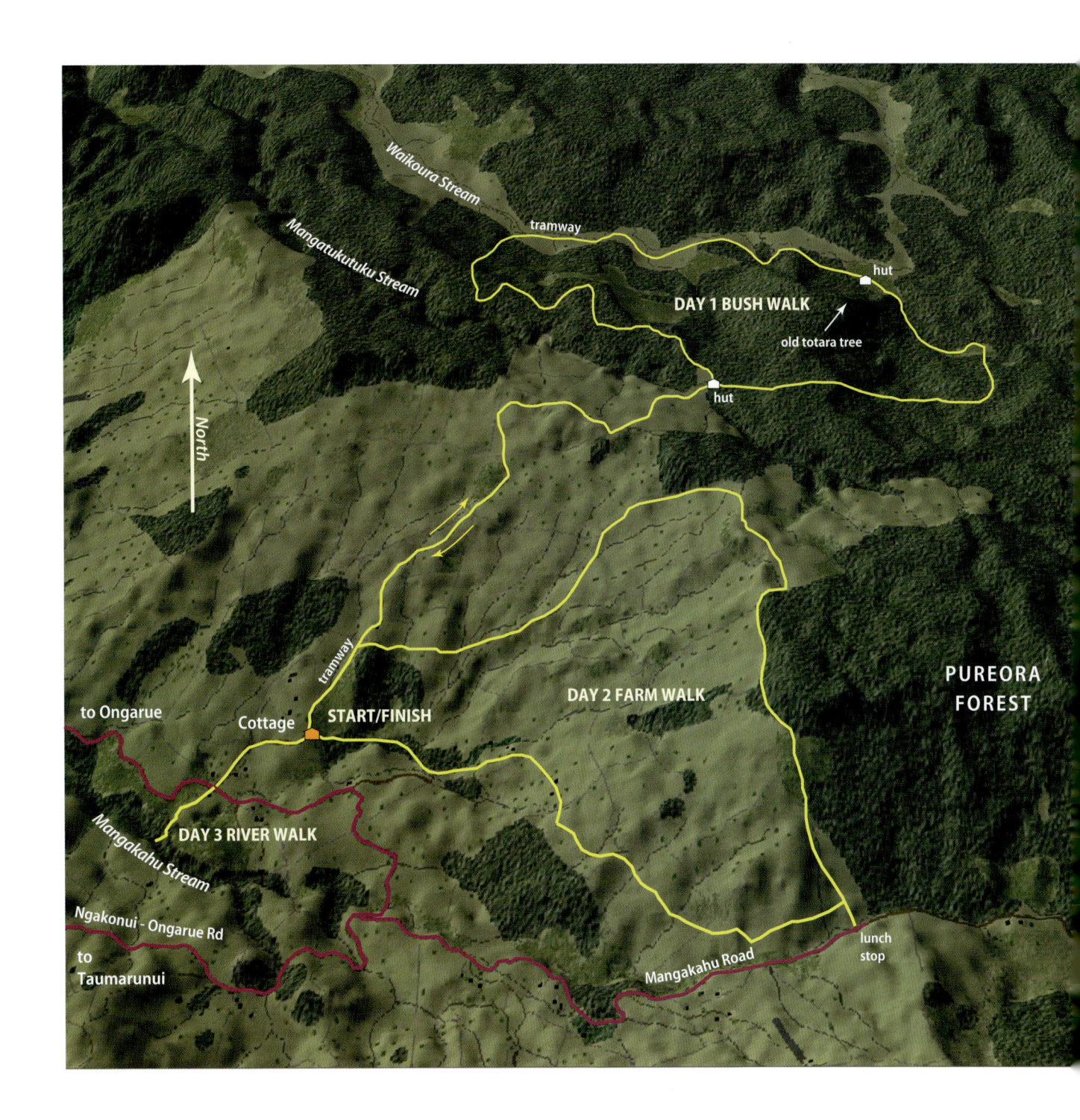

WALK WESTRIDGE, ONGARUE, NEAR TAUMARUNUI

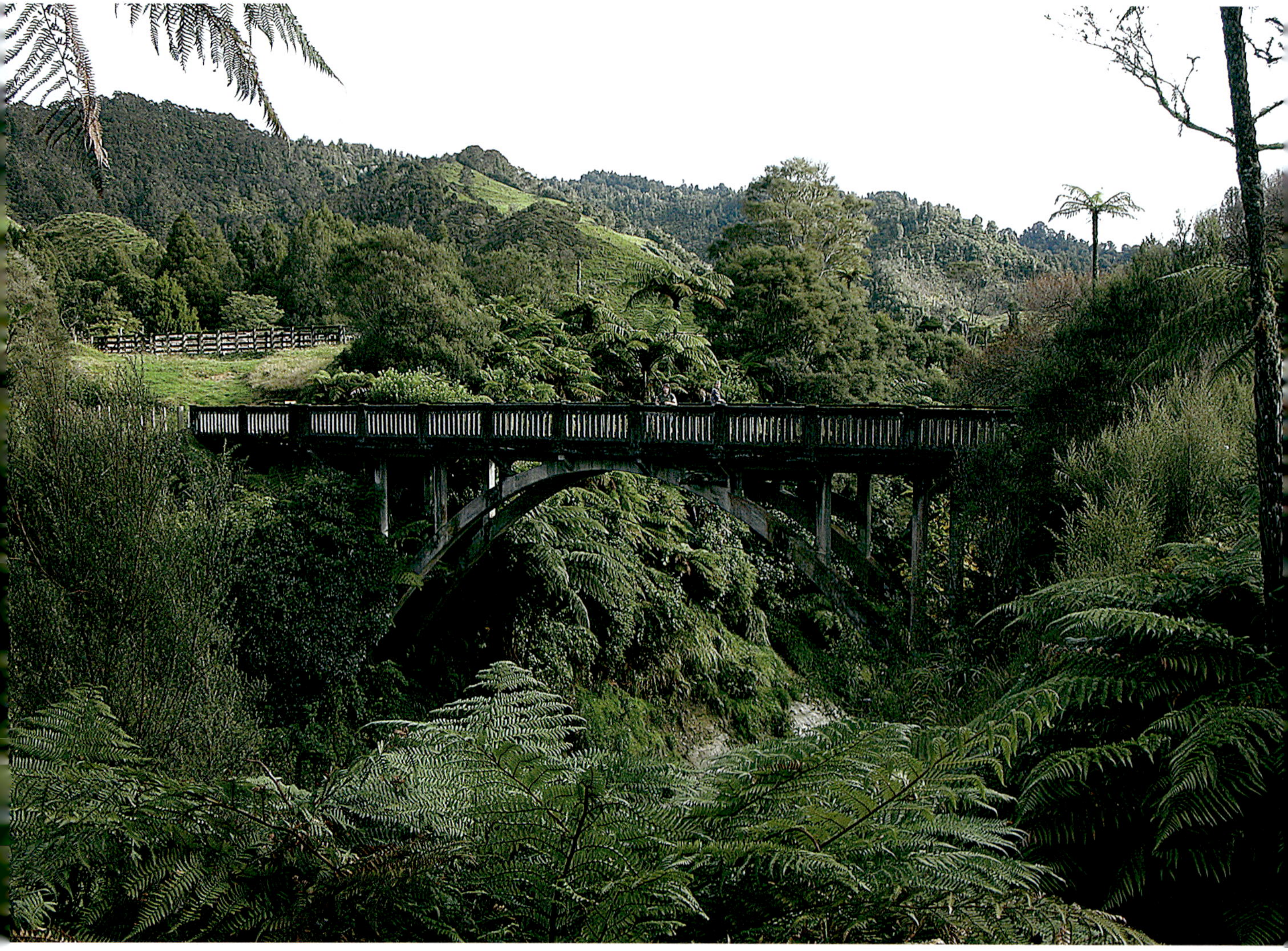

DOWN TO THE WALLOW
EASTERN TARANAKI EXPERIENCE, STRATFORD

For millions of years rain has lashed an ancient sea-floor basin in Eastern Taranaki, eroding the soft mudstones Maori named 'papa,' into a jumble of narrow, rugged ridges that signal their common origins with a near-uniform height. Streams carve crevasse-like gullies through the soft sediment in random, saw-cut patterns.

Rivers easily cut down through the papa so that even as the landmass rises they retain a relatively gentle gradient. And there is the mud—grey, like estuarine mud, and as sticky as cement. It is a mud that must have had settlers fresh from the trenches of the Somme wondering whether they had survived one hell on earth just to fall into another.

It is possibly not the sombre picture that Carol Digby of Eastern Taranaki Experience prefers to paint. Yet while there are many dry months during the September-to-May season of her three-day walk, a spell of heavy rain may create the appropriate conditions to fully appreciate the travails of those who have gone over this land before. Digby's outdoor adventures in eastern Taranaki are an aptly named 'experience' on which, after a downpour, you may need to dodge the mud on old and overgrown dray roads and thus be overwhelmed by the struggles of those who built them.

Digby seems an unlikely tourism entrepreneur and outdoors guide. Taranaki born and bred, she is slightly reserved without being diffident, has a rural sense of humour without being precocious and is, well, just plain nice—the sort of person you can always rely on to help out with school trips and the like. She has been tramping since 1996 and her outdoors CV includes membership of the Stratford Tramping Club, Forest and Bird and the Stratford Camera Club. She might well have ended up spending her spare time sizzling sausages for Stratford fundraisers had not a sailing trip to the subantarctic Auckland Islands in 1999 whetted her appetite for adventure. She has since trekked in South America, and completing the Tora Walk on the South Wairarapa coast inspired her to do something similar in her beloved eastern Taranaki backcountry.

Digby's Eastern Taranaki Experience stepped off in September 2001 and has been hugely successful, twice winning Taranaki tourism awards. The business is now run in conjunction with her husband, Dave Digby, a long-time tramper, mountain safety instructor and member of the Taranaki/Whanganui Conservation Board.

The trek begins at the couple's Stratford home before a short afternoon drive north on SH43, 'The Forgotten World Highway,' to the small farming settlement of Makahu and the first of two farmstays.

The Bridge to Somewhere at Aotuhia is a standard government design that stands as forlornly as the Whanganui River's famous Bridge to Nowhere.

This road between Stratford and Taumarunui is a drive through history, past small villages that once served coal mines, flour mills, railway workers and timber mills, and are now hosts to small clusters of long-closed shops. There are more than 30 large Heritage Trail signs along the way detailing and illustrating the history of the region. A typical sign reveals the grave of surveyor Joshua Morgan, who died on 3 March, 1892 at age 35, of suspected peritonitis, and whose legacy is many of the road routes through the region's maze of eroded papa. His widow died 50 years later in Murrays Bay, Auckland.

The 45-minute drive takes walkers to their first night's accommodation at the farm of Alan and Sylvia Topless. The couple has farmed there for more than 30 years, after Topless decided he preferred the outdoors to working as a joiner in New Plymouth. They have raised six children, now all grown up, yet still put in working-bee time at the local school, and wouldn't swap a day of their lives.

The hills in the near distance look impossibly steep, even though they are dotted with sheep. Topless explains it is actually good sheep and cattle country, so long as you keep it fertilised, as the process of erosion has left a good mix of hill country and fertile, sheltered flats. It says something about this farmstay that dinner may well be roast pork, a gift from elderly neighbours as thanks for some good-neighbourly chores Topless has done for them. And in the morning you are likely to wake to the 'awdle, ardle, oodle' of magpies and to the sporadic bark of farm dogs, impatient to be off the chain and at work.

The first day of walking begins in the Aotuhia Valley and traverses an 11 kilometre bureaucratic folly, the Kurapete Track. The route was surveyed in 1892 to join the 42 kilometre Matemateaonga Track, an old Maori foot track that traverses the narrow crest of the Matemateaonga

Whangamomona and its historic pub (middle left) are now best known for the biennial celebrations when the locals declare the village a republic. An old road built to link the village with farms in the Aotuhia Valley remains passable to walkers (right). Aotuhia Station dogs (bottom left) have their own neat and tidy hotel.

Range, one of the longest continuous ridges left by erosion, all the way to the Whanganui River. The Kurapete link was designed to give settlers in the Aotuhia Valley access to the transport highway that a fleet of riverboats made the Whanganui River. The boats could bring supplies to the settlers and take farm produce the other way. In 1920 relief workers widened the track into a dray road as far as Mt Humphries with the intention of creating a road link to Raetihi.

In February 1922 officials from the Public Works Department drove a truck as far as the Matemateaonga Track junction. That night a cloudburst sent sections of the fledgling road tumbling into the ravines beneath it and the project was abandoned.

The bush has reclaimed much of the track but it is a gentle gradient to the Matemateaonga Track, a small clearing and ideal lunch spot just short of Mt Humphries. The track is a National Walkway that has since been embraced by the Whanganui National Park, and there are 11 relatively flat and pleasant kilometres back to its beginning and a pickup to the second farmstay at the home of Don and Eila Hopkirk.

The Hopkirks are another of those hard-working farming couples who have been in the engine room of the New Zealand economy. They have now retired—son Will has taken over the farm—and Don and Eila's spacious home is given over to the most wonderful hospitality.

You would probably stay put for weeks if you could, so it is almost with reluctance that walkers return next morning to the Aotuhia Valley and the sad scene of rough, isolated land, settled mostly by veterans from the First World War on about 50 Crown-lease farms. Like their counterparts in the Mangapurua Valley on the other side of the Whanganui River, their labours proved fruitless and most walked off their land during the Depression. The last of them, Ted Wiley, stuck at it until 1942, but finally gave up when a huge flood destroyed what pasture he had and his road access out of the valley.

The Aotuhia School and Post Office have long gone, but a standard Ministry of Works concrete bridge over the Whangamomona River, built in 1937 when most of the farmers had left, remains. In deference to the famous bridge at Mangapurua, the Aotuhia structure is called 'The Bridge to Somewhere'—a reasonable appellation as it serves the Aotuhia Station, a single run covering part of the old settlement. And, until the flood that finally defeated Wiley, you could drive 20 kilometres into Whangamomona and drop your wool and cream at the railway station.

Tunnels cut through the papa rock (left) have been enlarged to cater for modern stock trucks by lowering the floor. The road leads to the home of Don and Eila Hopkirk (bottom right) and farm hospitality that tempts you to stay forever.

EASTERN TARANAKI EXPERIENCE, STRATFORD   65

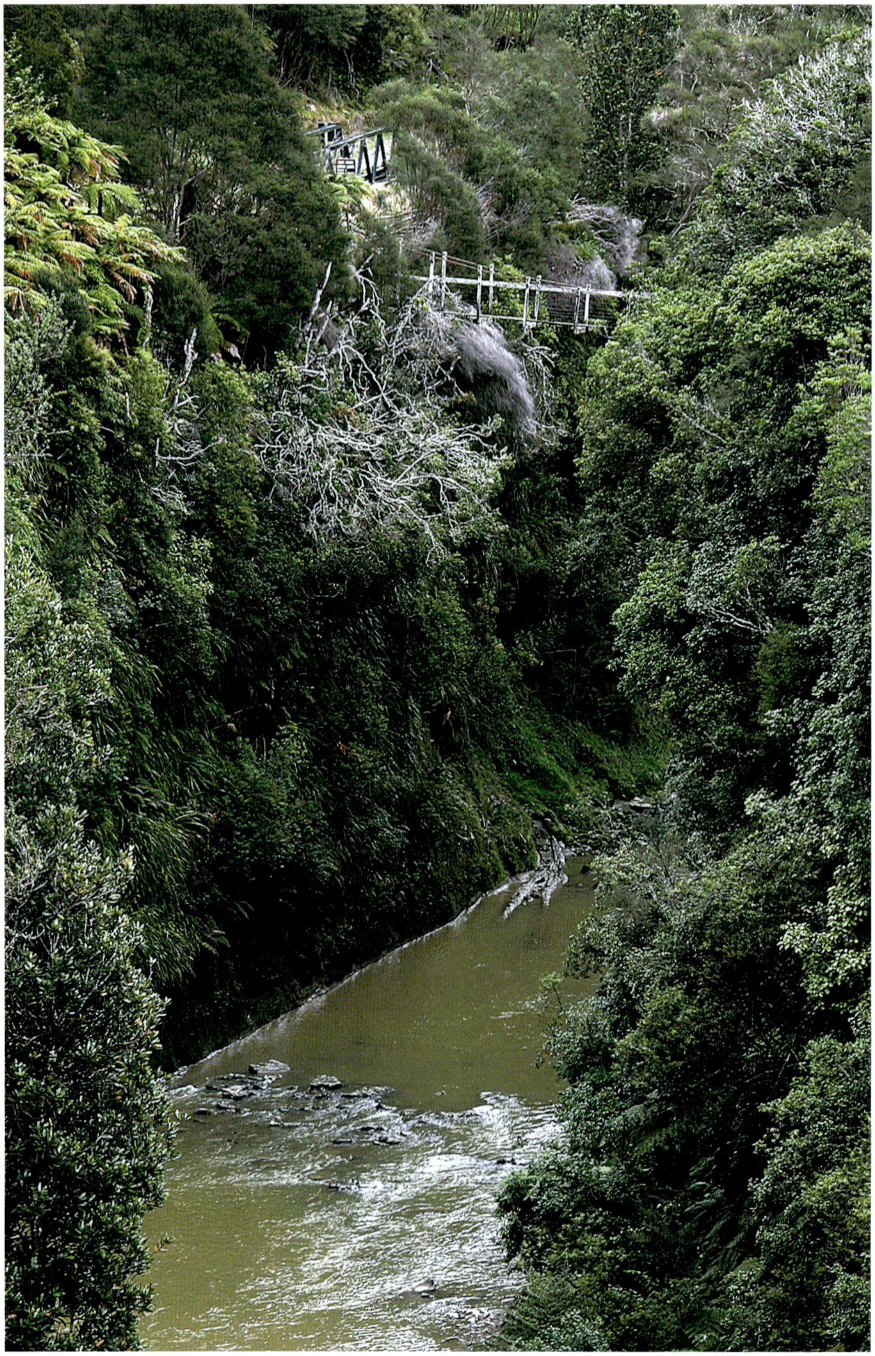

EASTERN TARANAKI EXPERIENCE, STRATFORD

Walkers use an old mahoe tree for a group photograph.

the locals celebrate the declaration of their own republic in January every two years.

In the morning you have a number of options—if you're 'walked out,' you can explore the historic town and its old buildings—banks, butchers, bakers, et al. If, however, you fancy some more tramping, there are a couple of walks to choose from—a three-hour bushwalk that the Digbys' clients often claim to be the best of the experience, or a walk in the Te Wera Pine Forest. The former trail follows a narrow ridge top and, at several places, the thin and sodden blanket of topsoil has slid away from both sides to expose a precipitous cliff of papa rock. Even a covering of mature bush can be defeated by this country. For either one, you then have time to enjoy a picnic lunch, before returning to Stratford in the mid-afternoon.

Time Three days, three nights
Length 30 kilometres plus
Type Bush
Start/finish Stratford
Catering Fully catered
Pack carry Yes
Special features Superb farmstays
Party number Up to 10
Accommodation Two nights farmstay, one night rural hotel
Bedding Provided
Season September to May
Further information www.eastern-taranaki.co.nz

A couple of years ago some four-wheel drive enthusiasts got the road passable again, putting in culverts and drains. Their efforts ensure the road is relatively dry much of the time, but if a major four-wheel drive run combines with rain, mountainbikers, horse-trekkers and walkers over the next few days will likely face a muddy mess—and get to understand what the settlers had to contend with. The old road passes through two tunnels and over several bridges as it follows the Whangamomona River, which feeds its muddy waters and debris into the Whanganui. The last night of the Eastern Taranaki Experience is spent at Whangamomona's legendary hotel, where the possum skin on the wall behind the bar is as big as a sheepskin, and

(P. 66) Muddy water spews down the Whangamomona River to the Whanganui River. Many walkers consider a walk in the pristine bush (p. 67) not far from Whangamomona to be the highlight of their trek.

EASTERN TARANAKI EXPERIENCE, STRATFORD   69

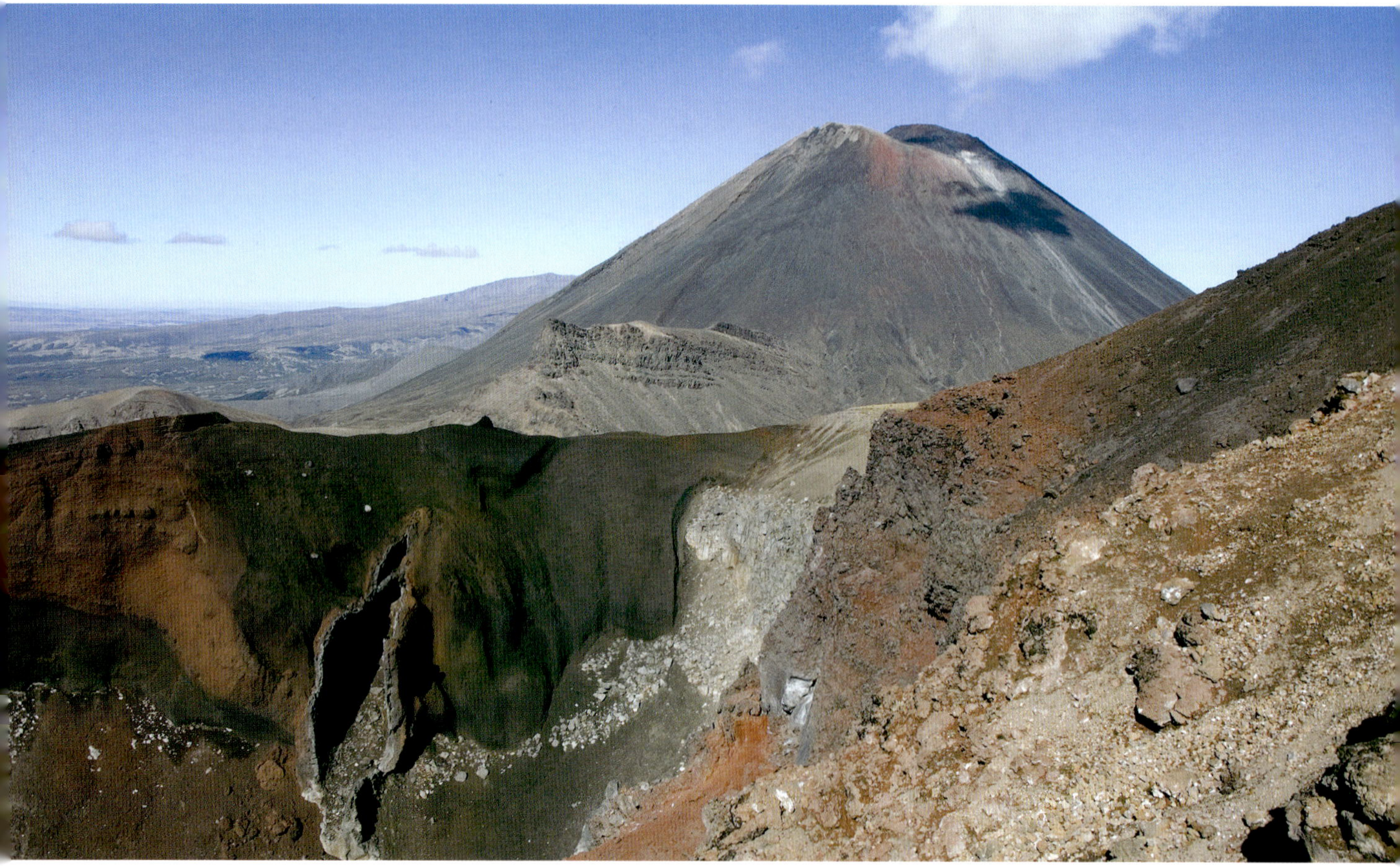

TONGARIRO TRUMPED
TONGARIRO ALPINE CROSSING AND OTHER WALKS IN TONGARIRO NATIONAL PARK

In 1894, Malcolm Ross, a journalist accompanying those who, a month later, would be the first to scale Mt Cook, was forced to turn his back on days of rain and wind, disconsolately reflecting that 'for a man with a limited holiday, mountaineering is a game of chance with the weather, and the weather generally holds three aces and a long suit.'

It still does; New Zealand's mountains stand isolated in the vastness of the Southern Ocean, exposed to whatever nature throws at them. Most people who have tried to snatch a summit within a set and limited timetable would attest to Ross's cruelly accurate observation. Even a seemingly modest foray into the alpine region such as the Tongariro Alpine Crossing, famed as the best one-day walk in New Zealand, is at the mercy of the weather. For the thousands who successfully make the crossing every year there are many hundreds whose long-planned weekend is sadly undone by capricious weather.

Listening to the tales of the disappointed set Rob Franklin and Hilary Sheaff, of the guiding company Walking Legends, to thinking how they could improve things. They reasoned that a four-day window should pretty well

The hellish volcanism of Red Crater and Mt Ngauruhoe, which were used to represent Orodruin, or Mount Doom, in the Lord of the Rings *movies, are on the Pacific Ring of Fire, a line of volcanic activity that stretches across the Pacific Ocean.*

guarantee a successful Tongariro Crossing, and, while there are no guiding concessions available on the crossing, a professional guiding company can do plenty to ensure an adventure is successful without having to hand-hold a client on the actual walk.

Sheaff, from Whakatane, and Franklin, from neighbouring Opotiki, met a few years back while summer guiding on the Routeburn Track. When Franklin's father died and Sheaff's brother almost lost his life in the same month, they returned to the Bay of Plenty to help their families. As a break from their duties, the duo walked the 46 kilometre Lake Waikaremoana Track, where something gelled between them. Perhaps they heard the singing and calling of the patupaiarehe, the fair-skinned people, or forest elves, that inhabit the mist-wreathed hills and valleys of the Ureweras. The upshot, anyway, was Walking Legends, a guided walking company with a DOC concession to operate guided and fully catered walks around Lake Waikaremoana and elsewhere in Te Urewera National Park.

But the duo are no strangers to Tongariro National Park, having worked for several seasons as custodians of the Rotorua Tramping and Skiing Club lodge in the Iwikau village on Mt Ruapehu. Expanding their business to include a four-day experience in the World Heritage-listed park was a no-brainer. As well as the Tongariro Crossing, there are many other adventure options in the park to soak up a few days, not least climbing to the Mt Ruapehu summit, which appeal to the sorts of people who don't like to waste any time in achieving their outdoor adventure goals. The Tongariro Experience provides the answer—the best the National Park has to offer, with logistical details such as food, accommodation and transport all taken care of.

Walking Legends' four-day Tongariro hiking programme is designed to be completely flexible so as to defeat the

The 'gut buster' from the Mangatepopo Valley to South Crater has been tamed by a formed stairway

weather, which may be unsuitable for a trek at altitude one day but fine the next. After being picked up from your accommodation in Rotorua or Taupo, the programme usually begins with one of the most delightful short walks in New Zealand—the track around Lake Rotopounamu, just south of Turangi on SH47. A lot of work has been carried out in recent years on the Rotopounamu Track, much of it by volunteers from the Tongariro Natural History Society, and if you want you can gallop around the lake in no time at all.

The track upgrading is no doubt environmentally friendly

and makes the walk more accessible, but to really enjoy this jewel of a walk you need to take your time, even if it is now along metalled paths and not over a carpet of beech leaves and a washboard of tree roots. The towering rimu and kahikatea, red beech, maire and matai forest that surrounds the lake—the largest in Tongariro National Park—is renowned for its birdlife and birdsong, as long as you take time on the track raceway to listen to it.

In the heavy bush, damp and shady here, drier there, are pigeons, shining and long-tailed cuckoos, kaka, robins, bellbirds, tui, fantails, tomtits, wax-eyes, grey warblers and riflemen—a prolific natural aviary that will often descend from the treetops to investigate those who pass beneath, particularly if they have come prepared with a squeaky bird caller. It is not unusual to be able to lure four different species onto the one branch just a couple of metres from you.

A picnic lunch beside Lake Rotoaira is followed by a walk to the remarkable redoubt at Te Porere, built by Maori leader and warrior Te Kooti. That these complex earthworks beside the headwaters of the Whanganui River were rapidly thrown up by pick and shovel is as astonishing as the outcome of the battle in 1869 that saw Te Kooti and his followers put to flight by the attacking British soldiers.

Nature can take the credit for the earthworks of the next adventure, a two-hour loop track to the Taranaki Falls starting from Whakapapa village. These are splendidly captivating falls by any measure, but what sets them apart is that the Wairere Stream that feeds them with cool snowmelt water plunges over the schisms of an old lava flow, wearing the rock as smooth as marble.

Accommodation for the night is the Rotorua Tramping and Skiing Club lodge, where the evening meal is sumptuous. It is early to bed though, because Rob Franklin will want you away before daylight to get a head start on the dozens of backpackers who are shuttled to the beginning

At Ketetahi Shelter (middle) the daily busload of backpackers who have 'ticked off' the Tongariro Alpine Crossing (top) wait for a shuttle pickup. Despite warnings of changeable weather in the alpine environment, many still make the trek ill-prepared. Te Porere Redoubt (bottom) is a marvel of engineering.

of the Tongariro Crossing, in the Mangatepopo Valley, every morning.

The early part of the walk, the climb up to South Crater between Mt Ngauruhoe and Mt Tongariro, used to be called the 'gut buster'. Now, though, while the altitude gain remains the same, the track is made on a wide boardwalk and moderately inclined zig-zag bench track that people of average fitness tend to find effortless. Often the early start will bring the added bonus of the rising sun turning the mountains a stunning pink.

When the weather is perfect it would seem quite impossible to lose the snail trail that gets marked across the route by thousands of feet all summer. But the weather can be deceptive and frequently catches out the ill-prepared. Once you reach the highest points of the track you are likely to be exposed to a cooler breeze that at times can become dangerously chilling—not that you would think so from the young mob chasing your tail. Despite the warnings from DOC, many on the Tongariro Alpine Crossing—a 'must do' for adventurous tourists—seem dressed for an expedition to the shopping mall not an 18.5 kilometre alpine trek.

Having successfully completed the Tongariro Alpine Crossing, walkers are rewarded for their efforts with a formal dinner at the Tongariro Grand Chateau, although the dinner may instead be scheduled for the final evening. The following morning, it's time to attempt the climb to the summit of Mt Ruapehu. It's a civilised start to the day, however—no pre-dawn rises for this one— as you use a chairlift to take you up to make the attempt. In good weather the climb to Dome Shelter at 2672 metres is pretty straightforward and many people make it each summer. But, as an added precaution, walkers on the Tongariro Experience are accompanied by Paul Ratlidge, an alpine guide with local company, Adventure Headquarters, for the five-and-a-half-hour return trip. At the summit of the North Island's highest mountain, you can enjoy the impressive views of the central plateau and all its volcanoes.

Taranaki Falls (top) is a modest excursion, but it is a stiff climb to reach Dome Shelter (bottom) on one of the Mt Ruapehu massif's seven summits

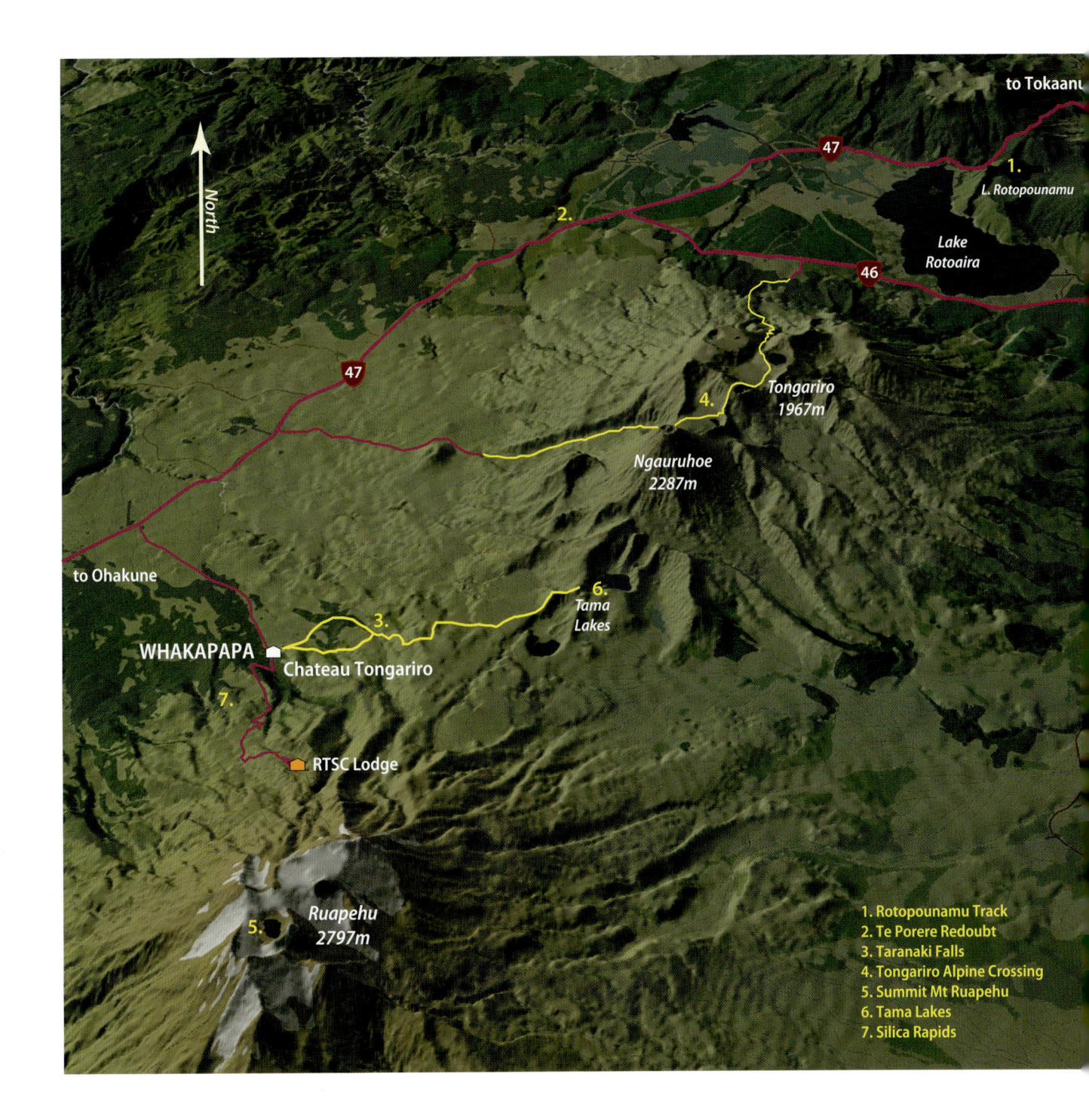

TONGARIRO ALPINE CROSSING AND OTHER WALKS IN TONGARIRO NATIONAL PARK 75

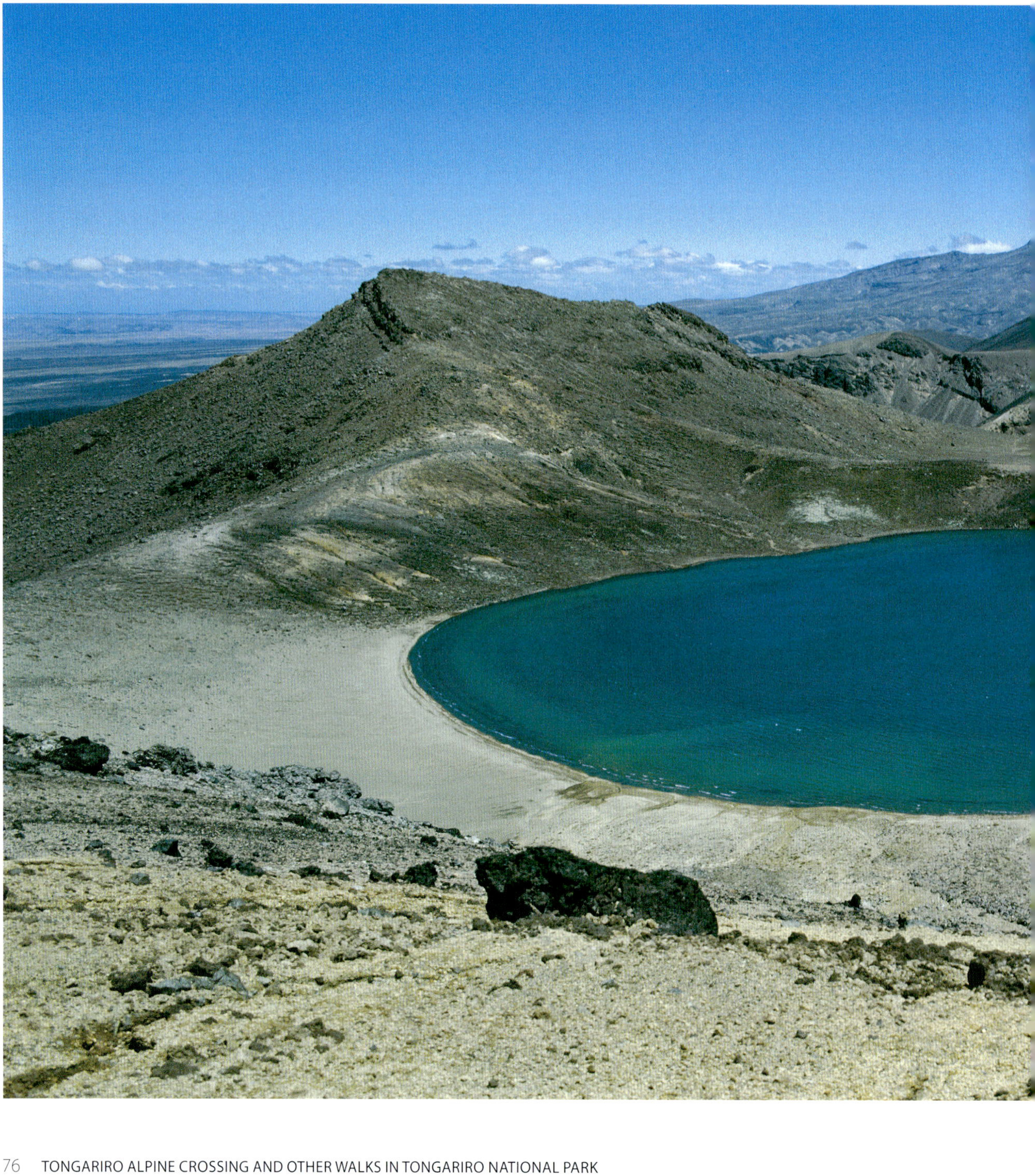

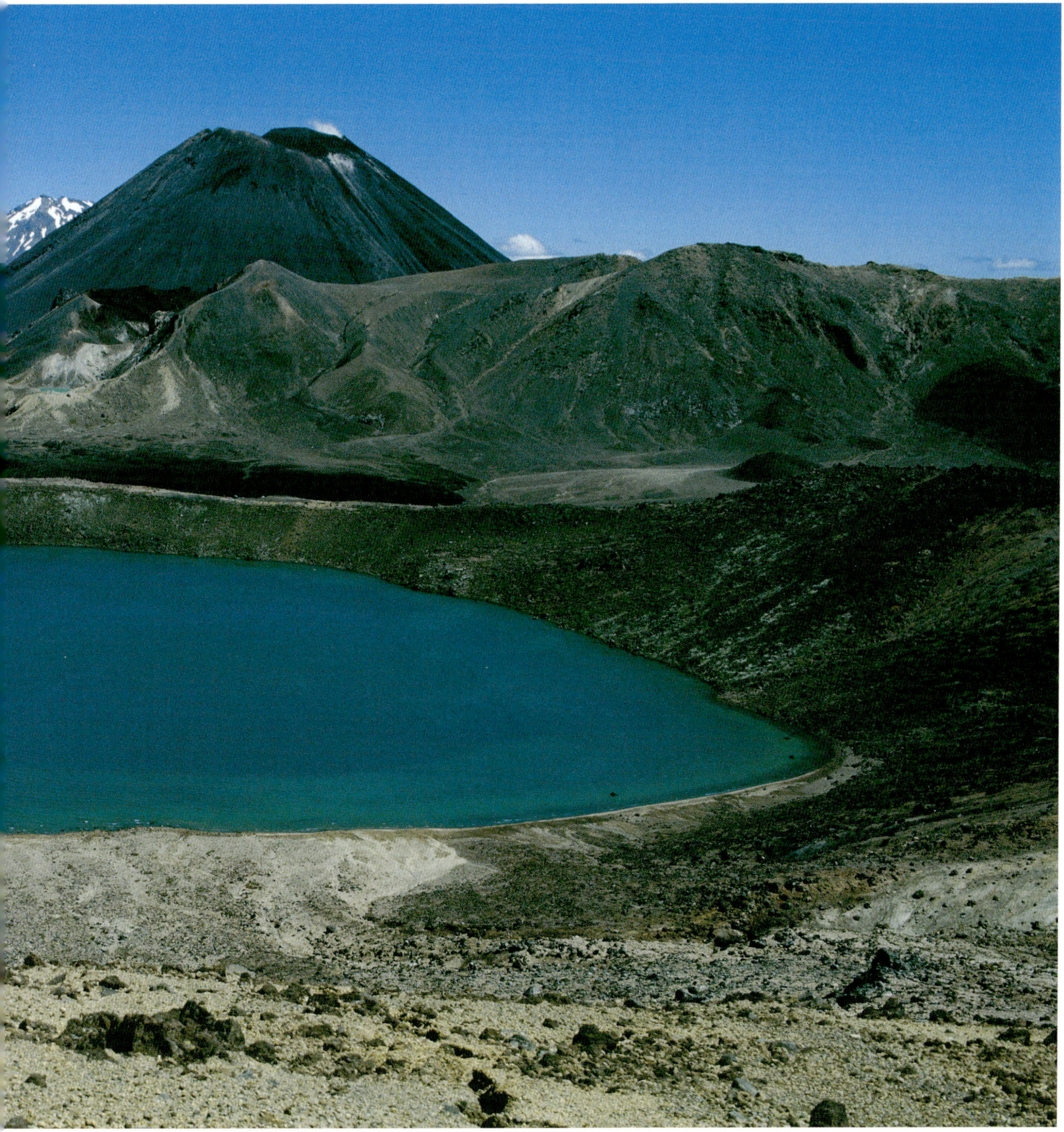

The mature native forest (above) around Lake Rotopounamu, once a volcanic crater on the side of Mt Pihanga, provides a stark contrast on the Tongariro Experience to the ash- covered summit and steaming crater lake of Mt Ruapehu. The massif is softened by the pink glow of dawn (top).

If you fancy a more relaxing day you will have the option of heading down to the Whakapapa Visitor Centre to do some of the shorter walks in the area, perhaps to the Tama Lakes on a section of the Tongariro Northern Circuit Track. Dinner that evening is another Franklin treat at the ski lodge, washed down with a good choice of wine. The final day it's time to pack up and, if you're still in the mood for some walking, you can do the short trek to Silica Rapids before departing for Taupo and Rotorua by late afternoon. However, with the Tongariro Crossing and Ruapehu summit under their boots, some customers bail for an early start home. They are busy people; time to move on.

Time Four days, three nights
Length Flexible itinerary, depending on weather
Type Native bush, alpine trek
Start/Finish Rotorua or Taupo pickup
Catering Yes
Pack carry Not required
Special features Superb mountain views, alpine trek in safety
Party Number Maximum 14
Accommodation Fully featured lodge
Bedding Provided
Season November to April
Further information www.walkinglegends.com; www.adventureheadquarters.co.nz

(Top) Above Ketetahi the view stretches across Lake Rotoaira and Lake Taupo as far as the Bay of Plenty

(Pp 76–77) Blue Lake, with Mt Ngauruhoe behind and Mt Tongariro to the right, on the Tongariro Alpine Crossing.

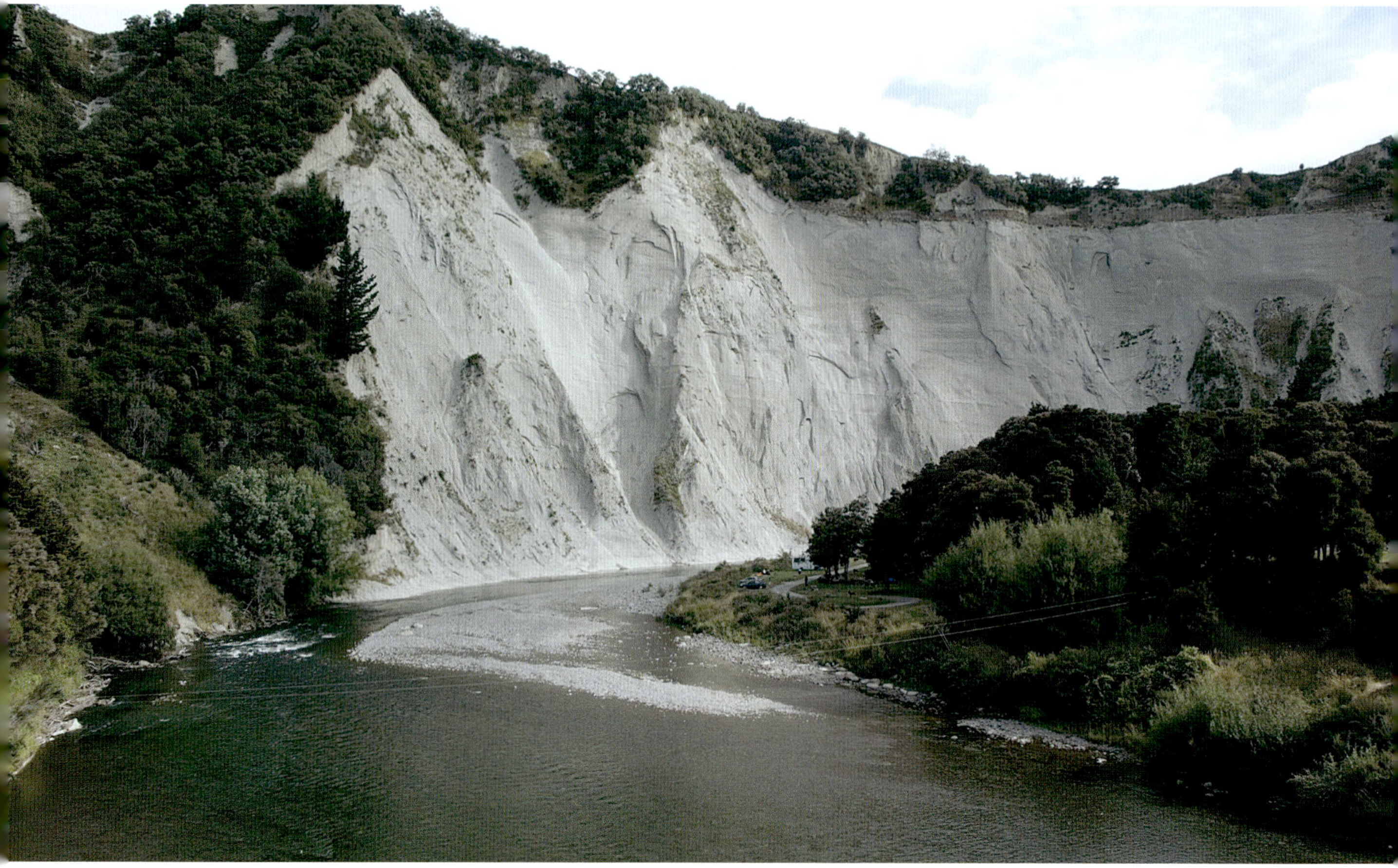

A RIVER RUNS THROUGH IT
KAWHATAU VALLEY WALK, MANGAWEKA

When SH1 was re-routed past Mangaweka, just south of Taihape, in the early 1980s it could have easily blanked the small town off the map. Fortunately, some places can't be ignored. A brightly painted vintage DC3 aircraft ensures motorists know it's Mangaweka they are zooming past, while the smart ones will take time to stop in the old town and enjoy the new art and craft galleries housed in historic shops.

Nature has gone one better in providing historic attractions though—the enormous white papa cliffs, left by the Rangitikei River as it carved through the Mangaweka Gorge, are a timeless and unmistakable reminder of the town the highway now bypasses. The cliffs are worth a detour, because if you follow the road that leads to them you will soon pass more spectacular white papa bluffs and come to a byway gem, the Kawhatau Valley. It is a relatively narrow valley reaching far back into the Ruahine Range and carrying the Kawhatau River down its centre until it joins the Rangitikei River.

If you were to paint a pastoral river valley, it would likely look much like the Kawhatau. The river terraces are given over to green and neat pasture with generous plantings of stately poplars to hold the deluge-sensitive papa soil in check—although sodden slabs still slip off the hills in the worst of storms. Where the bowling-green flat terraces

Spectacular papa cliffs on the Rangitikei River at Mangaweka are a signpost to the junction of the Kawhatau River and its gem-like valley.

stop abruptly, the land rises on a not-too-onerous slope to the skyline. If you climb to these ridge tops, the views are perfectly splendid, with the snow-covered summits of the Mt Ruapehu massif easily visible to the north, and the riven Ruahine Range far in the hazy distance to the east.

This is the Rangitikei, a region described by its mighty river that sits neatly between the Whanganui hinterland and Hawke's Bay. The Ruahines bound it to the east, the Kaimanawa Range to the north and the flat lands of the Manawatu to the south. The geography of Kawhatau Valley seems almost a miniature version of the entire region. What better place then to set up a three-day walk over private land?

The Kawhatau Valley Walk is a three-day walk that, like the valley itself, is an eclectic blend of the Rangitikei—rich river-flat farmland, hillsides with commanding views of the hinterland, rivers of wild trout, and warm, rural hospitality. And what better people to do it than two neighbouring couples who, apart from their shared passion for farming and the rural bliss of the Kawhatau Valley, seem to have been absorbed from quite different neighbouring areas.

Bunny and Kristin Gorringe have farmed their property for several generations, and the homestead and its extensive and colourful gardens are reached up a long metalled drive, flanked by mature oak trees, that winds its way through lush pasture. There won't be many New Zealand farmers with an agricultural degree from Oxford University among their credentials, nor with such long service in the public arena of catchment boards, rural advisory committees and such like.

Beyond the homestead lies the tidiest collection of farm buildings and equipment you are likely to see. Each piece of farm machinery is precisely angle-parked along the drive, while fenceposts yet to be used, along with those being recycled, are neatly stacked. All the tools in the large equipment shed hang in their respective spot, with not a bit of clutter on the swept concrete floor. Bunny Gorringe doesn't wear a suit and tie during the long hours he puts in daily around the farm, but you would hardly be surprised if he did. The clean paddocks are grazed by a mainly Perendale flock, each animal carefully selected by a man with a keen and experienced eye for perfect conformation.

The Gorringes' neighbours, Ruth and Jim Rainey, have the ruddy, windburnt look that seems to give them away as farmers. Actually Jim Rainey was born and brought up in the city but he would look out of place in a suit and tie. He abandoned the city to go shepherding around the country, and ended up working on one of the Massey University farms in the Manawatu until he and his Massey-educated wife Ruth bought their Kawhatau Valley farm in 1994.

The two couples soon became friends, and Ruth Rainey and Kristin Gorringe enjoyed doing things together. On their way to a residential cooking course Kristin couldn't stop talking about the Tora Coastal Walk in the Wairarapa she had just done. By the time the pair got home, not only had they both honed their cooking skills but they had planned a rural walk of their own in the Kawhatau Valley.

Once they'd made the decision to set up the walk,

Dipping sheep on the Gorringe farm in the Kawhatau Valley may be mechanised but remains an intensive chore. Bunny Gorringe (top and left) likes his sheep as clean as his pasture.

things began to happen, and on the Gorringe farm the old shearers' quarters, built in 1904, were beautifully restored and refurbished as accommodation for night one of the package. In fact, the place has so much character that you may well be tempted to put your feet up and blob out for a few days to the rural sounds of sheep, dogs and the distinct magpies' call.

But you are here to walk, and the first day of 22 kilometres is along the valley's southern ridgeline, along a trail that passes a remnant of the native forest that once clothed the area and has now been fenced off from stock. The forest on the steeper land was cleared by partially cutting the larger trees and then felling a large tree in a key position at the top of the hill so that it would knock over all the trees below like dominoes. The fallen trees were burned and grass was sown in the warm ash. Now Bunny Gorringe plants groves of poplar trees to try and control erosion. The track rises gently to a trig at 716 metres from where you can see Mt Ruapehu standing majestically to the north.

Below is The Green Trout, a lodge purpose-built by the Raineys on a terrace above the Kawhatau River for walkers—and for trout fishers. Jim Rainey is a keen fisher, voluntary ranger and guide, and runs guided fly-fishing trips on the Rangitikei River tributaries, using a raft or helicopter for access.

Even if you are not into trout fishing, there can be few more pleasant ways to spend an evening than on the deck of The Green Trout, looking down into the Kawhatau River and listening to Rainey's fishing yarns. You might also be tempted to order a meal from Ruth Rainey. She took that cooking course to heart and now supplements the farm income with a small catering business.

Day two is an 18 kilometre loop that at first continues along the valley's southern ridge, before dropping down to the valley floor to an outdoor education centre that was developed by the Taihape Rotary Club when the Kawhatau

If you forget your walking pole there is no shortage of spares you can use on walks in the Kawhatau Valley (pp. 84–85), a pastoral river valley that could have been created by a landscape artist.

KAWHATAU VALLEY WALK, MANGAWEKA

KAWHATAU VALLEY WALK, MANGAWEKA

86 KAWHATAU VALLEY WALK, MANGAWEKA

Primary School was closed in 1987. The young children of the valley may have been the losers when the school closed, but those of the region were definitely the winners as this is now a quite perfect site for a school camp. Through the grounds and beyond the classrooms that have been converted into bunkrooms lies the upper Kawhatau River. Its braided reaches, with just a few shallow crossings required, will take you back to The Green Trout, although you may well be tempted to first stop for a swim in one of the many quiet pools.

Take one old shepherds' hut (bottom left) and the old shearers' quarters (top left), add some TLC, elbow grease and imagination, and you have wonderfully rustic accommodation that will send anyone to sleep utterly relaxed. Lush river terraces (above) produce healthy grain crops.

KAWHATAU VALLEY WALK, MANGAWEKA

The braided reaches of the Kawhatau River make for easy walking, while trout feed and rest in the many deep pools.

On day three you have the choice of three routes back to the shearers' quarters on the Gorringe farm. You can walk back down the southern flanks of the valley a little beneath the ridge traversed on day one, and through pleasant patches of retained bush and poplar groves, for up to 15 kilometres. You can take a more direct route towards the end and shorten the trek to 10 kilometres. A middle option of about 7 kilometres is to continue down the Kawhatau riverbed, water levels allowing. Cool off with a dip in a river pool and keep an eye out for trophy trout—but don't let Jim Rainey catch you trying to hook one if you don't have a fishing licence. Better to buy a licence and return to The Green Trout on a fishing trip and have Rainey guide you to the secret spots on the Kawhatau.

Time Three days, three nights
Length 37 to 40 kilometres
Type Farmland, native bush, river flats
Start/finish Kawhatau Valley Rd
Catering On request
Pack carry Yes
Special features Trout fishing
Party number 10 to 12
Accommodation Fully equipped lodges
Bedding Pillowcases, duvets, towels. Linen extra
Season Labour Weekend to end of April
Further information www.kvw.co.nz

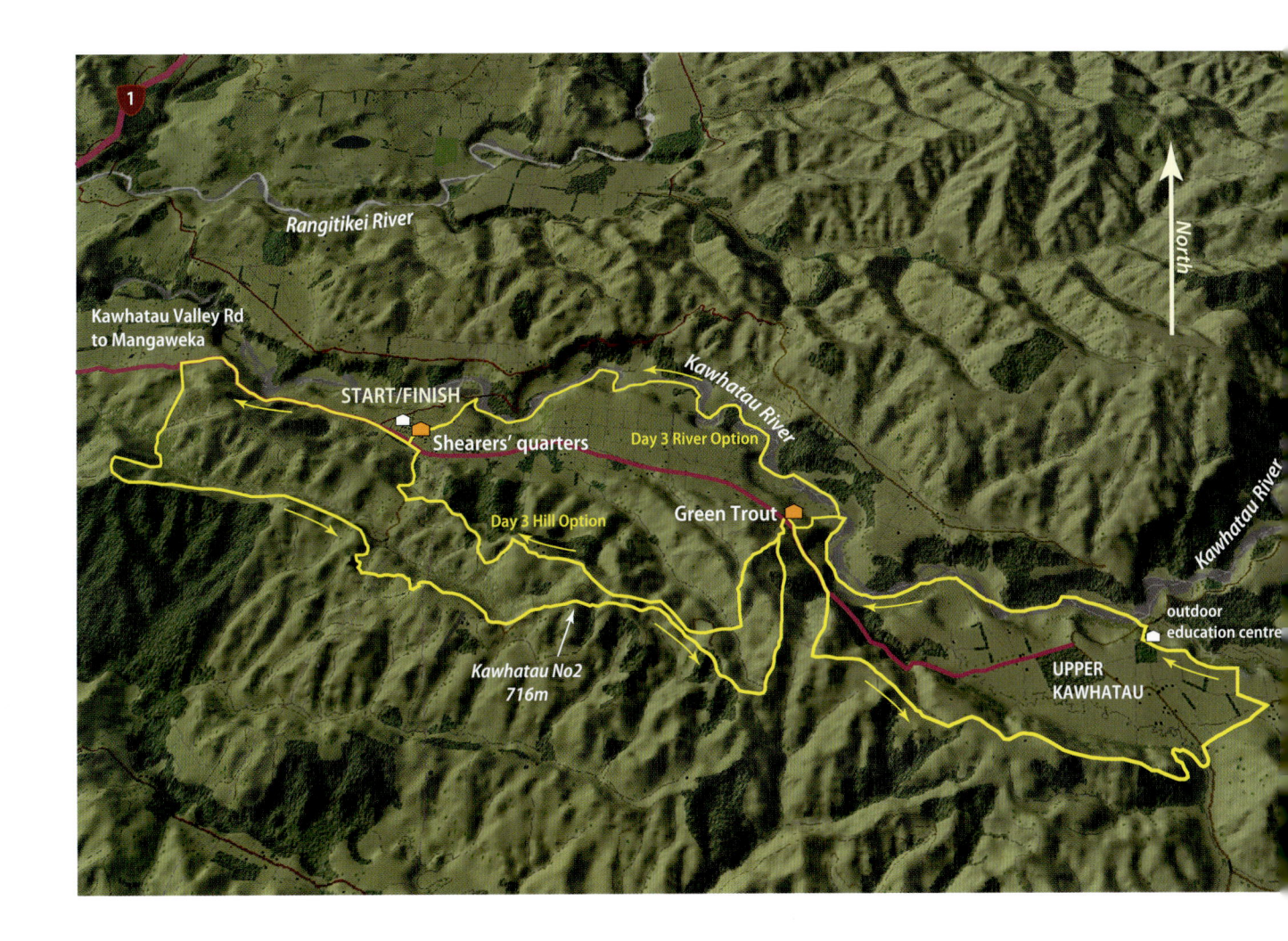

KAWHATAU VALLEY WALK, MANGAWEKA 89

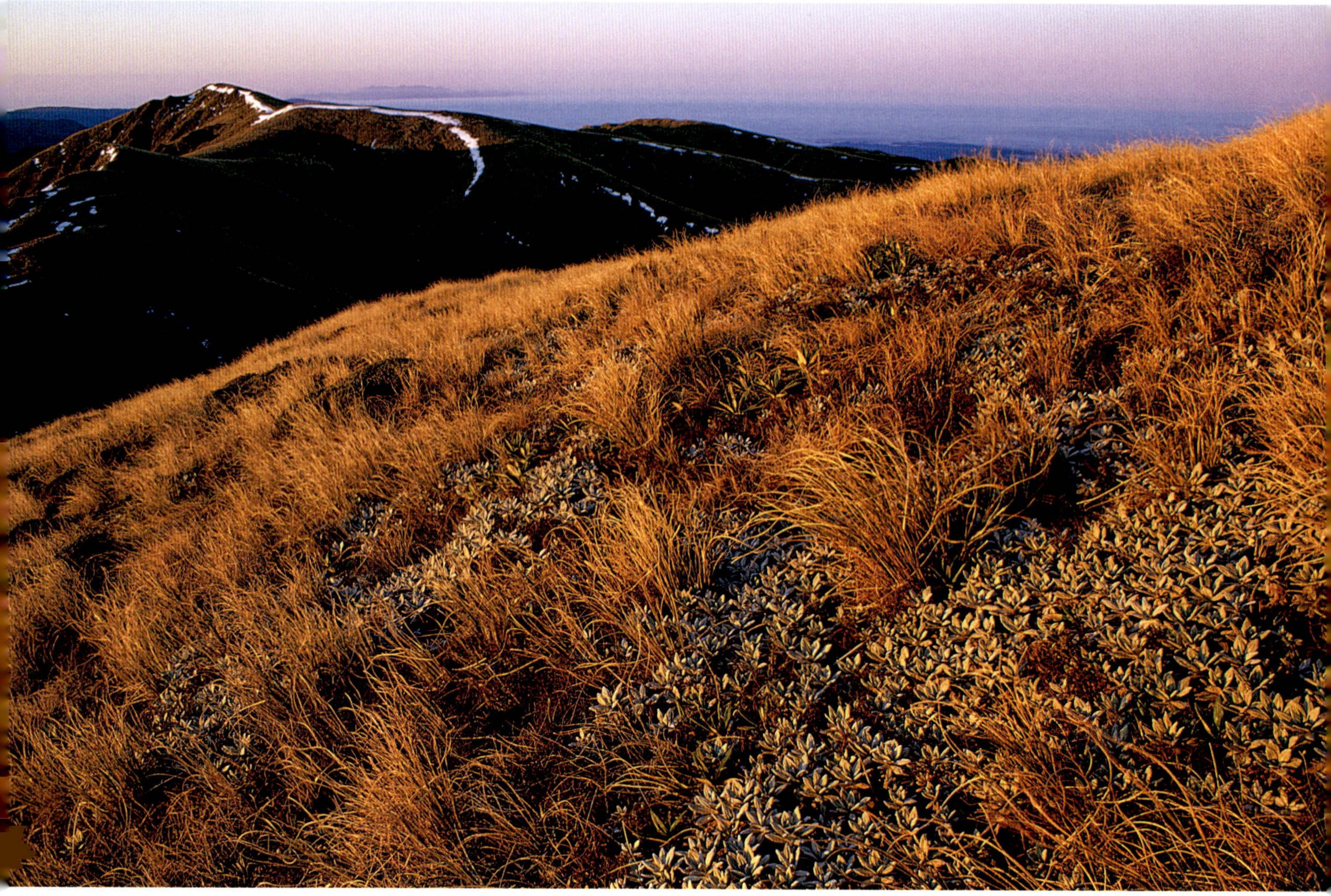

FARMSTAY COMFORT

WEKA WALKS, MT HUIA FARM, RUAHINE ROAD, MANGAWEKA

If a day in the fresh country air is good for you, then several days should be a real tonic. So thought Neil and Virginia Travers when they set up a farmstay operation in a cottage on their farm, Mt Huia—a 351 hectare hillcountry farm in the Ruahine Valley, nine kilometres from Mangaweka.

It is now sheep and cattle country but wasn't always so. When the native forest was first clear-felled from the valley and its tops in the late 1800s—taking the last huia birds with it—the denuded land was mostly cut into 80 hectare holdings and used for dairy farming. It was a bad call; the Ruahine Dairy Factory built in the valley closed at the turn of the twentieth century and the small farms began to amalgamate and turn to sheep and cattle farming. Not all succeeded. One holding ended up run down and under the care of the old Lands and Survey Department, which spruced it up, carved the property into three and sold the pieces off by ballot in the early 1960s. One of those was Mt Huia, which the Travers bought in the 1980s and where they later established their farmstay.

Selwyn Hodd had won the ballot for one of the trio of properties back in the 1960s. However, the farm was a bit

Ruahine Forest Park provides a rich backdrop to the Weka Walks. Subalpine tussock and white daisies adorn the slopes of the Whanahuia Range.

odd in that the new house and 12 hectares were on one side of the Mangawharariki River and the rest of the land was on the other. Hodd sold to a neighbour who sold the 12 hectares and house to pay for a bridge to the rest of the farm. When this amputated holding, just across the road from Mt Huia, came up for sale again, the Travers couldn't resist adding it to their existing property. Their old farmstay cottage had by then passed its use-by date, but their interest in rural tourism remained and they wanted to venture into the private walking business. Given the location of Mt Huia, near the western foothills of the Ruahine Range, establishing a walking programme based around the Hodd Cottage accommodation was a natural development.

Such serendipity couldn't have fallen on a more suitable couple. Neil Travers is a born and bred farmer, who went to Massey University to hone his rural skills; Virginia Travers is a trained dietitian, long-time foodie, and stalwart of the regional tourism industry, serving on the committee and as chair of the local District Tourism Organisation, Rangitikei Tourism.

92 WEKA WALKS, MT HUIA FARM, RUAHINE ROAD, MANGAWEKA

This is a rural region with a startling amount of activities for tourists, from the varied attractions of Taihape, the country's 'gumboot capital,' to a range of adventures, such as jetboating, rafting and trout fishing on the Rangitikei River.

But if speeding down rivers and fishing aren't your thing, there could be no better way to really enjoy the ambience of the rural heartland than to blob out on a working farm with 2940 sheep and 280 cattle for company, and enjoy three day walks from the Travers' farmstay at Hodd Cottage. It is the ideal base—the cottage is a pleasant, typical 1960s three-bedroom weatherboard home set on a tidy lawn and gardens. It would look at home in an older city suburb, but urban homes are rarely found in such a private and idyllic setting. The Mangawharariki River, which flows down the Ruahine Valley to join the Rangitikei River near Mangaweka, twists and turns through a deep gorge just below Hodd Cottage's rear deck, carving Kainui Bluff out of the limestone. The bluff is a commanding gothic backdrop in the late afternoon sun as you relax on the deck sampling some of Virginia Travers' home-made goodies and a glass of wine.

A track leads down to the river and a secluded picnic area with several swimming holes where the solar-heated and naturally filtered water is perfectly clear and you don't need to worry about a bathing costume—unless you feel modest about sharing the pool with a trout or two. Relaxing in your own private gorge is a peaceful way to spend a few hours. Wander along the river and you will see the sign of fossils in the rocks and perhaps the fallow deer which have made their home on the riverbanks. You can self-cater, have your dinner delivered, or be hosted at the Travers' own diningroom table. Fresh country air tends to lead to healthy appetites.

At Hodd Cottage you get the daily newspaper delivered,

Mature beech trees (right) in the Ruahine Forest Park (top far left) provide a walking counterpoint to the pasture on Mt Huia station (bottom far left). At Hodd Cottage (left) you can even have the newspaper delivered.

and can feed the hens in the cottage henhouse and collect your own eggs for breakfast, if you want. An indication of how you can spend your time is given in the various comments of the visitors' book. One example, from BK, Hong Kong, reads, 'We mustered, sheared, swam in the river and ate the most delicious farm sausages and gourmet dinner from Virginia—and all in a day and a half!'

The first day's walk is around Mt Huia farm itself. It is primarily a pastoral walk on a loop of about four hours—leaving plenty of time to relax in the Mangawharariki River pools—but the farm also contains many small stands of native trees, some in larger reserves and conservation pockets.

The geology is particularly fascinating. On the bank of a farm road, at more than 500 metres above sea level and in easy sight of the Ruahine Range to the east, are clusters of fossilised shells that were once in a primeval sea before being squeezed into the Rangitikei hillcountry about five million years ago. A narrow, steep-sided valley reveals what Neil Travers calls his water-level marker. A distinct line along the face reveals the level at which water is moving through the limestone and feeding the grass below it. The valley faces also reveal the slip damage caused during a storm in February 2004, when the saturated soils just could not hold any more water.

The second day walk, over the neighbouring Glen Tui farm of Kevin and Karen Waldron, and the Department of Conservation's 283 hectare Titirangi Reserve, takes a full day. The bush-clad reserve reaches to a ridge at 675 metres. On the other side of the ridgeline fence is the farm of Bunny Gorringe, below it the Kawhatau Valley, and in the far distance the Ruapehu massif. Walkers on the Kawhatau Valley Walk (page 81) traverse the same ridgeline. The reserve is a block that was balloted off for farming in the 1800s but never cleared of its forest cover because the owner decided the land was too steep and hard to get to. Eventually the block became a farm-locked island of unspoilt native podocarp forest, with a dense canopy and a rich undergrowth of

The track to Rangiwahia Hut crosses one of the Department of Conservation's more romantic structures—a Japanese-style footbridge.

mosses and lichens. It is now a reserve maintained by DOC and cleared of possums. It has been described as one of the best examples of lowland forest in the North Island.

The return route is along the reserve fenceline until you drop back into Glen Tui farm—but not before reaching a knob from where, on a clear day, you can see north to Mt Ruapehu, west to the Tasman Sea, south to Kapiti Island and east to the Ruahine Range. Parts of the walk are steep and challenging, and by the time you get back to the comforts of Hodd Cottage you will have some idea of the effort spent on clearing the land for pastoral farming—and the wisdom of one 'land owner' who decided not to.

The third day walk is a Ruahine Forest Park classic, a trek through beech forest and tussock country to the Rangiwahia Hut. It starts at a DOC car park about 20 minutes' drive along the Ruahine Valley from Hodd Cottage, and from there the trail is gentle and well maintained, although there is a need to detour around a massive slip. A feature of the track is a Japanese-style bridge across a 70 metre deep gorge, through which runs a fresh bubbling mountain stream.

The 12-bunk Rangiwahia Hut is above the bushline and

Time Three days, three nights
Length Various
Type Farm, native bush
Start/finish Hodd Cottage, Mt Huia
Catering Yes
Pack carry Not required
Special features Cosy farmstay
Party number Six to eight
Accommodation Fully equipped lodge
Bedding Supplied
Season Labour Weekend to 30 April
Further information www.mthuia.co.nz

After a hard day's walking there is nothing nicer than to return to Hodd Cottage and walk down to the river for a cooling and utterly private swim. It is so inviting that it is best you take your beer or wine with you.

96 WEKA WALKS, MT HUIA FARM, RUAHINE ROAD, MANGAWEKA

WEKA WALKS, MT HUIA FARM, RUAHINE ROAD, MANGAWEKA

sometimes, in the winter after a good snow dump covers the tussock, is a favoured destination for backcountry skiers. The original hut on the site was built by the now disbanded Rangiwahia Ski Club in 1938. The club once had 80 members but nowadays the snow cover is usually marginal.

It is an easy one-day walk to the hut and back but Weka walkers, should they want to, could get a DOC hut ticket and spend the night at Rangiwahia Hut. Still, it is probably more tempting to turn around and return through the beech and kaikawaka forest to Hodd Cottage, where another visitors' book statement reads: 'Tramping deluxe style! Very well organised and great hospitality and surroundings. SM, Auckland.' Enough said, really.

The Rangiwahia Hut in Ruahine Forest Park began life as a ski club hut and is still used by backcountry ski tourers. (above).

Kainui Bluff (pp. 96–97) provides a distinctive backdrop to Hodd Cottage. The virgin bush of Titirangi Reserve is at top left.

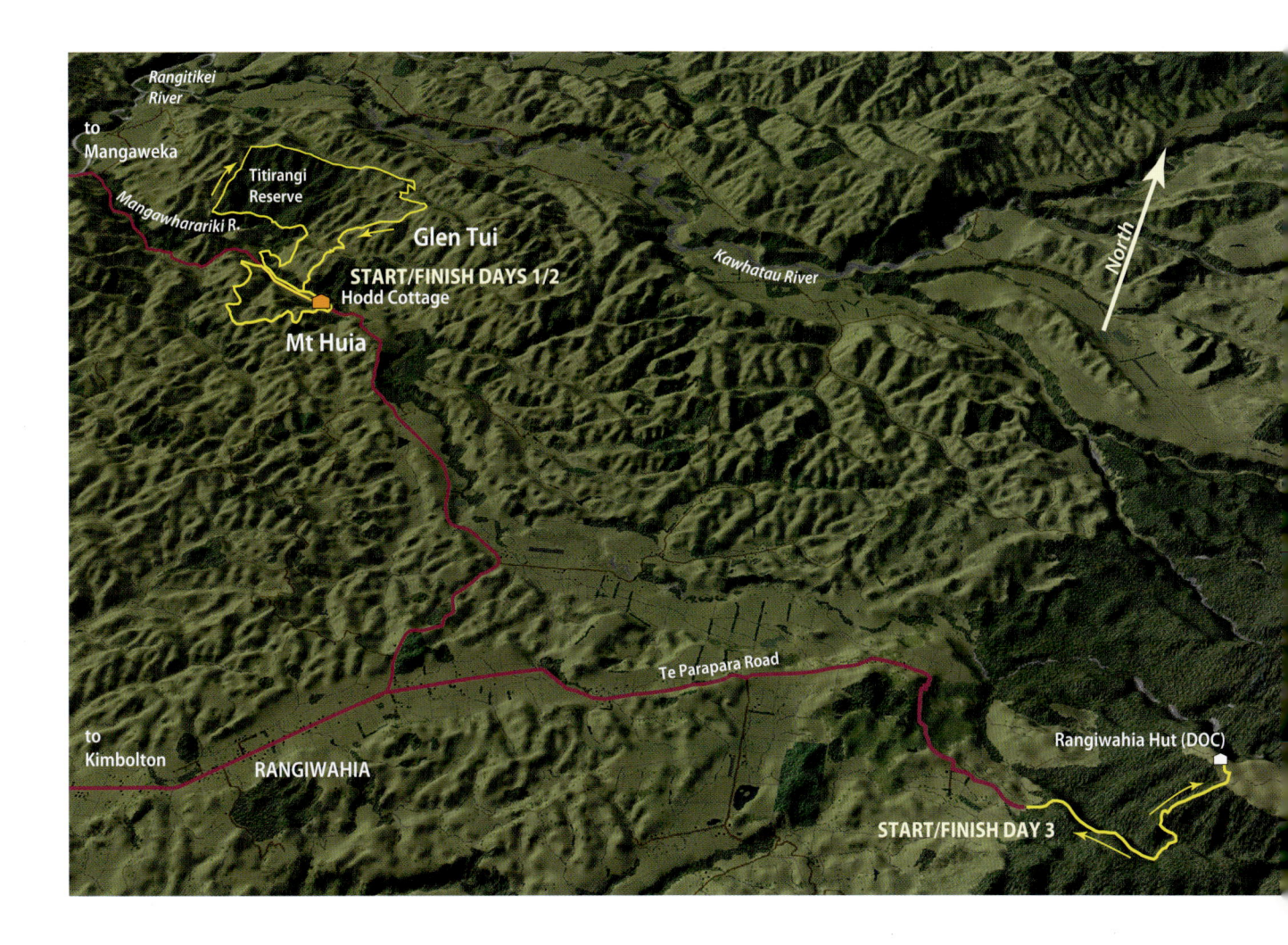

WEKA WALKS, MT HUIA FARM, RUAHINE ROAD, MANGAWEKA   99

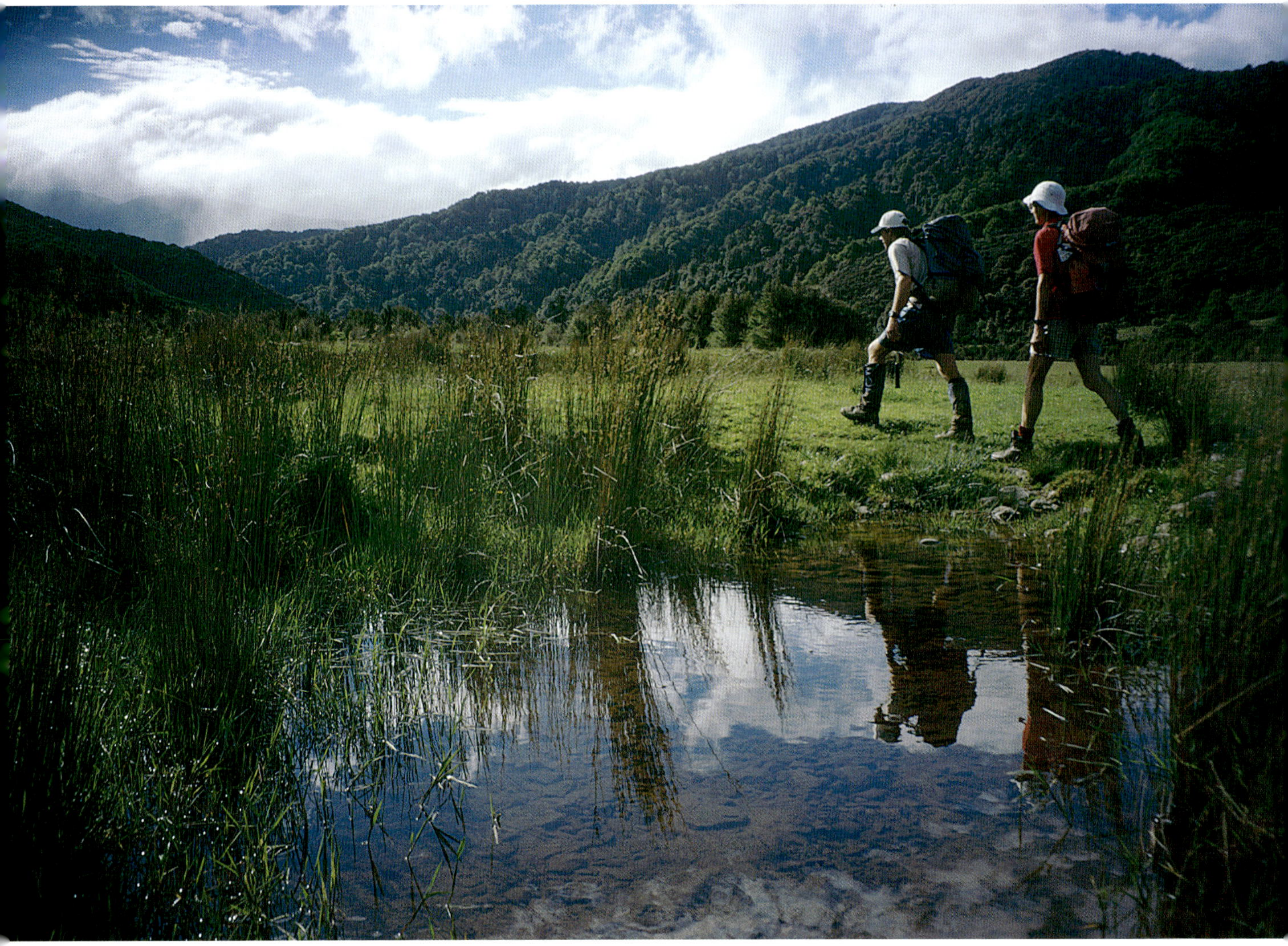

TAMING THE TARARUAS
TARARUA WALK, MASTERTON, WAIRARAPA

There are trampers and there are Tararua trampers. The former don boots, shoulder a pack and trek around much of the New Zealand wilderness. The latter, personified by the legendary 'Man of the Mountains,' John Pascoe, consider them to be mere walkers. Real trampers scamper up and down the wilderness ramparts that form the northern bulwark to the country's capital.

Tararua trampers are a tough breed, and they need to be. The ranges that sort the men from the boys are steep up and steep down. And when you do gain the tops, you are likely forced to seek refuge in a Department of Conservation hut that will be as welcome as the Ritz but, of course, will not be anything like it. Such is the fearsome reputation of the Tararuas that most mere mortal trampers rarely bother to visit the Forest Park. But as with most things, there is another side to this classic mountain range—a yin to the yang. The softer side lies to the north and east, protected from the fearsome southerly and south-westerly weather.

It is the face of the Tararuas that generations of trampers from Masterton have enjoyed and probably wondered just what all the macho fuss was about their outdoors playground.

Among them is Wairarapa farmer, Shona Inder, and a couple of mates from the Masterton Tramping Club, Dayle Lakeman and Jason Christensen. Around the turn of the nineteenth century Inder's great-grandfather, Thomas Wyeth, ran three farms in the Wairarapa and operated a sawmill at Mt Bruce, near the present site of the national bird sanctuary north of Masterton. Wyeth milled matai and rimu hewn from the bush and dragged to his mill by bullock and horse-drawn trams. One of his employees was Jason Christensen's great-grandfather.

The genesis for a Tararua tramp with a bit of comfort was when the Masterton tramping trio were following a track along the Ruamahanga River, north of Masterton, and came upon a small and derelict farmhouse on an old Wyeth property, now owned by Inder's cousin. The dilapidated two-roomed cottage, built in 1890, once housed a family of seven, and over the years had been used as a musterers' hut and more recently by hunters as a bush camp.

It was in a sorry state but it gave Inder the idea of turning her passion for tramping into a business. Her tramping partners joined her in setting up Wairarapa Wilderness Adventures, and the three of them set about turning the hovel into a place they could use as an accommodation base for a wilderness experience.

The cottage had no road access so everything required for the major makeover had to be carried in from the road

Can the turbulent Tararuas be more peaceful than in the Ruamahanga Valley?

end 3 kilometres back down the Ruamahanga Valley. The big stuff came in by helicopter, or over a steep hill by quad bike and farm trailer. The transformation included re-piling, installing a wood stove and gas burner, building a spa, adding a conservatory, a new bunkroom and a separate four-bunk chalet. By the time the tramping partners had finished, Reef Hill Hut, named after a nearby hill that the folks in Thomas Wyeth's day wrongly thought contained a large reef of gold, was a bush retreat that could make even hardened Tararua trampers salivate. It has cold running water, flush toilets, an outdoor hot tub and nothing but the bush for a neighbour. And there is only one rule at Reef Hill Hut—guests are not allowed to lift a finger.

Reef Hill Hut, with the Ruamahanga River flowing just below it, is in such a tranquil yet stimulating location that it was the obvious place for the tramping partners to begin their business. They started by offering a 24-hour wilderness experience, based on a gentle 45-minute walk beside the river and a night in the hut in relative luxury with nothing but the birds, bush and river.

The Ruamahanga is a short stroll from the hut, along a trail lined with ferns and beech trees, and once there you can swim in its pools, sunbathe on the large, grey boulders, or cast for trout. When you return to the hut there will be good food, wine, cheese, and a wood-fired hot tub waiting. Relaxing with a book or playing fun games rounds off the evening. And you don't get to leave until you have consumed a gargantuan breakfast and a morning tea of fresh scones.

From there, developing the three-day Tararua Walk and its sibling, the three-day Te Mara Walk, both making use of Reef Hill Hut, was a natural progression for Shona, Dayle and Jason.

The first day of the Tararua Walk starts at the end of the Mikimiki Valley, which follows the Mikimiki Stream west of SH2 into the Blue Range and the foothills of the Tararua Range. The 8 kilometre DOC track is in the Tararua Forest

The Raumahanga River is both tranquil and stimulating—a place to swim, sunbathe and cast for trout.

Park and follows an old logging tram track north to the next east-flowing valley stream, the Kiriwhakapapa Stream.

It takes about three hours through beech and kamahi forest and, along the way, passes relics of the old logging days—lengths of rusted tram tracks and what is left of an old boiler that once powered the winches the loggers used to haul logs out of the bush and lift them onto wagons.

Shona Inder meets her walkers with tea and snacks at the Kiriwhakapapa Shelter at the end of Kiriwhakapapa Road, before escorting them for another couple of kilometres to home for the night, Daniell's Hut, owned by Gary Daniell, mayor of Masterton. It was built on a 260 hectare family

A holiday home with a difference—Reef Hill Hut is on the edge of a forest park.

holding 40 years ago when the three Daniell brothers were given £100 between them by their sawmill-owning father. The boys used the money to build a retreat in the bush.

Walkers on the Te Mara Walk are ferried from the Kiriwhakapapa Road end to the top of a hill a little way back down the road and the start of a short farm track that leads down towards the Te Mara wetlands and the night's accommodation at Te Mara Lodge. The privately owned wetlands are protected by a Queen Elizabeth II Trust covenant. In the

TARARUA WALK, MASTERTON, WAIRARAPA

morning they follow a trail through the wetlands, along the Te Mara Stream, until they meet an old logging track and converge on the route taken by Tararua Walk trekkers from Daniell's Hut. To the west lie the brooding heights of the Tararua Ranges, the ridges probably stung by north-west gales and rolling cloud, while trekkers on the Tararua Walk and the Te Mara Walk are in the sheltered lee. The destination for both walks is a night in the luxury of Reef Hill Hut but there is a little surprise before they get there. An old scrub-cutter's hut has been turned into the Wilderness Café, which provides a cuppa that walkers invariably claim is among the best they have ever had.

There is no shortage of inviting accommodation at Reef Hill Hut—comfy beds, good home-cooked meals and places to relax. The Te Mara Wetlands (top right) are protected by a Queen Elizabeth II Trust covenant. The Ruamahanga River (pp. 106–107) is a cold but peaceful place to swim

TARARUA WALK, MASTERTON, WAIRARAPA

TARARUA WALK, MASTERTON, WAIRARAPA

It is just a short walk from the café to the luxuries of Reef Hill Hut, a cold swim in the Ruamahanga River, or a hot spa under the stars sipping wine, resting weary muscles and listening to the moreporks.

Day three is a casual 3 kilometre walk—over the hills or along the Ruamahanga River—back to where cars have been left in a secure car park.

Last word to one of those Tararua hard men, John Rhodes: 'I could get used to this sort of walking,' he wrote in an article for the Federated Mountain Clubs bulletin.

Time Three days, two nights
Length About 25 kilometres
Type Bush walk
Start/finish Mt Bruce, SH2
Catering Yes
Pack carry Yes
Special features Bush and bliss
Party number Eight
Accommodation Fully serviced huts
Bedding Sleeping bag required
Season October to end May
Further information www.tararuawalk.co.nz

Tararua Walk partners, Shona Inder, Dayle Lakeman and Jason Christensen, have a wonderfully wry sense of humour that comes from long years of tramping with the Masterton Tramping Club. So a shelter at the head of the Waipoua Valley, where walkers can stop for a brew, is the Wilderness Café, while down at the Reef Hill Hut you can lie back in a hot spa while Inder serves wine and nibbles.

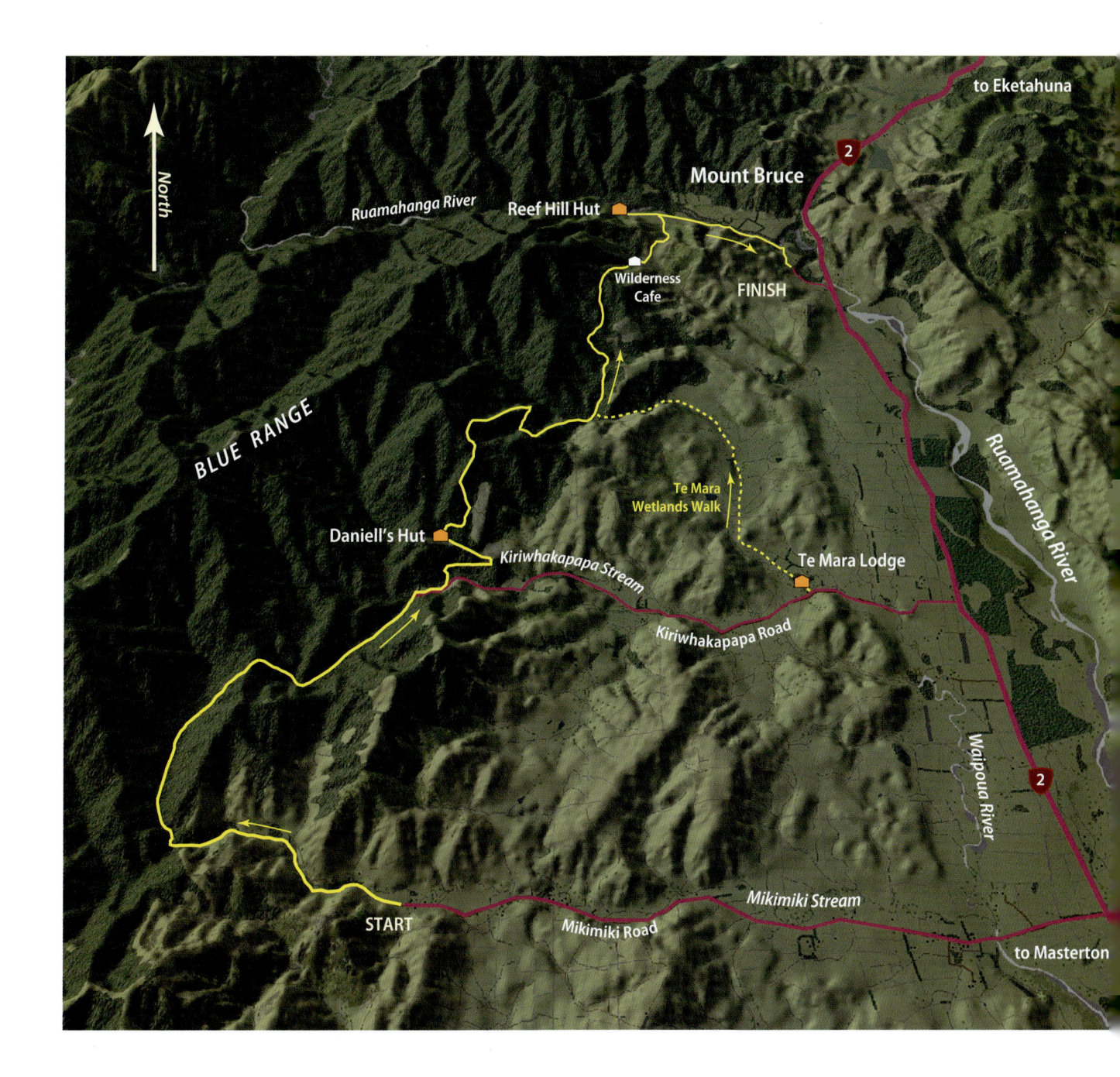

TARARUA WALK, MASTERTON, WAIRARAPA   109

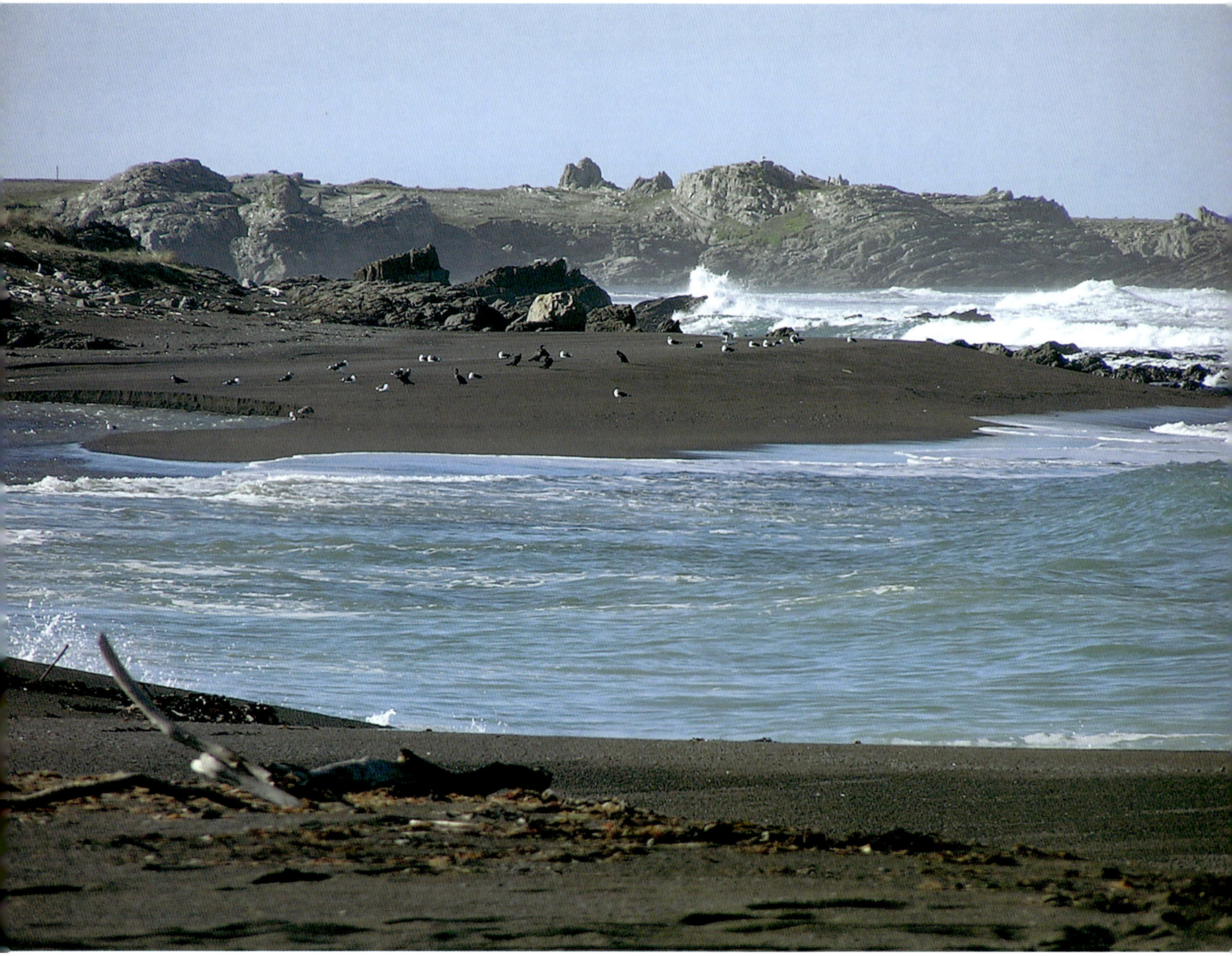

MARCHING ON ITS STOMACH
TORA COASTAL WALK, SOUTH WAIRARAPA

The name sounds like the codeword for the Japanese attack on Pearl Harbour. In fact, it is a corruption of the Maori 'Te Oroi.' But among New Zealanders with an interest in the outdoors, Tora means just one thing—a three-day walk on the South Wairarapa Coast that is a must in any tramping CV.

Saying you've completed the Tora carries much the same import as telling people you've notched up the Milford or the Routeburn. That a private trek should be mentioned in the same breath as any of the country's nine public 'Great Walks' is testament to the wholly satisfying experience that comes from completing this three-day walk through bush, river valley, and the wild and rugged Tora Coast, 34 kilometres south-east of Martinborough.

You could say the Tora Coastal Walk had its genesis in the mid-nineteenth century, when the Crown bought a huge parcel of land from the Maori living on this bleak coast and then on-sold it to European settlers. One of the biggest beneficiaries was the Riddiford family. Daniel Riddiford had already acquired more than 12,000 hectares in the 1840s and driven sheep around the coast from Wellington to stock them. By the time his son Edward died in 1911, the Riddiford holding had grown to more than 28,000 hectares, earning Edward the title of 'King' from the Maori community. The estate was divided among his three sons, and at the end of the Second World War, the 5417 hectare Tora Station, belonging to Eric Riddiford, was sold to the Government for rehabilitation farms. It was then divided into 10 units of equal stock-carrying capacity and settled in 1952.

Fast forward a few decades and the 1000 hectare Little Tora unit, farmed by the Elworthy family, has a visitor. Myles Handyside used to be a shepherd on the old Tora Station when it was farmed by the Riddifords, and his son, David, is taking him on a trip down memory lane. David and his wife Sally are two of the principals behind the Kaikoura Coast Track, the second private trail in the country. 'You could do something like that here,' he tells Jane Elworthy and her friend and neighbour, Jenny Bargh, who with her husband, Chris, farms another 650 hectares of the old Riddiford land.

The two neighbours walked the Kaikoura Coast Track to see what David was on about, and they must have been impressed because in October 1995 the Tora Coastal Walk became the first private trek in the North Island and just the third in New Zealand. It is a distinctive mix of regenerating native bush, farm land and stunning coastal views of the wild Wairarapa coast. With more than 1000 people walking it

The Wairarapa Coast is both wild and beguiling, a place to watch nature in the raw.

each year, it is one of the most popular ventures of its type in the country. The track is well maintained, easy to follow and peppered with markers and points of interest. The three accommodation cottages are comfortable, fully featured and with all the essential mod cons, television excepted; this is a time to get away from the outside world.

But there is one thing in particular that sets the Tora walk apart—food. All three days are fully catered and the Tora cuisine is now legendary. All dishes are home-made, mostly with locally sourced fresh produce. On the Tora Coastal Walk the Martinborough region's reputation for fine food and dining passes the ultimate test—satisfying people who have walked for their supper.

You arrive at the first night's accommodation—The Little Tora Outstation, once the Tora Station musterers' hut—and pinned to the kitchen wall is a handwritten note from Kiri Elworthy, Jane's daughter-in-law, who has now taken over from her, with the dinner menu. In the fridge, just waiting for you to pop on the gas barbeque, are lamb chops in a herb and red wine marinade, new potatoes, broccoli, a Greek salad, roast pumpkin and chick pea salad with a sun-dried tomato dressing—and sticky date pudding with butterscotch sauce to follow. Bon appetit! You may have to cook it yourself but as it transpires there are huge benefits to that. By the time the meal is ready to serve, total strangers have chatted over the barbeque, shared table-laying duties, sought advice from each other on the best way to do this or that, and are likely sharing each other's wine. If ever there is a way to break the ice among a group thrown together on an outdoors adventure, cooking a Tora meal has to be one of the best. After that, getting the dishes done is a breeze.

The walk is pretty damn good too. Day one is over Little Tora and out to the coast, a 13.3 kilometre walk that takes from four to five hours. But those who think they have more

The wreck of the Opua *is a sign of the coast's potential fury, but at the Nissen Huts (bottom left) it is easy to lie back as though in the most benign spot imaginable.*

cobwebs to shake off can begin with a 6.5 kilometre loop in the other direction, which will add about two and a half hours to the day. The Whakapata Loop follows a benched farm track and includes a kilometre through native bush, as well as passing through a lovely stand of mature beech trees. The walk proper follows Tom's Creek for about an hour before beginning a steady climb through regenerating native bush of black beech, matai and kahikatea, to a high point on the ridge at 273 metres. This is the Wairarapa coast and it often gets windy at these exposed heights.

The Oterei River provides the route back into the hinterland.

Just a few ridges back on the way to the Outstation are the seven large wind turbines of the Hau Nui (Big Wind) wind farm, which supplies the southern Wairarapa with about six per cent of its power needs.

On the Tora Coastal Walk it is worth getting a bit of wind in your face when you can get the sort of 360-degree views that you do from this point. And if the view and breeze take your breath away, which they may well do, just a little way off the ridge is an old goat shelter where you can catch your breath and pause for lunch. The rest of the trail, now in Hiwikirikiri farm, follows the undulating ridge to the Witches Hat, an appropriately named little 'peak' that rewards those who scramble up it with exhilarating views of the coast. Below is home for the night, the Nissen Hut, or more accurately a collection of Nissen huts. They take their name from Peter Norman Nissen, a British army engineer who designed these half-round, corrugated-iron buildings as temporary military shelters. When the Tora Station rehab farms were sold to ex-servicemen they each came with one or more army-surplus Nissen huts to use as farm buildings. On the beach front of Hiwikirikiri farm, several Nissen huts were joined together, lined and fitted out as a homestead, with more than enough rooms to serve as a lodge for Tora walkers during the walking season.

The sumptuous food waiting for you at the Nissen Hut will have been prepared by Kiri's sister-in-law and neighbour, Kathryn Elworthy, a former Masterton radiographer, and now partner in the business.

Day two is as easy as you care to make it, and there are a number of options, from a one-hour, 4 kilometre walk, through to five hours and 16 kilometres. You can wander down the coast to the wreck of the *Opua*, a coaster that in 1926 mistook the lights of Tora Station for those of Wellington. The *Opua*'s rusty boiler in the surf is barely worth the walk, but the coast itself and the seal colony at Manurewa Point are—and you will get an entirely different perspective when you retrace your steps and then continue on to Te Awaiti Bay and the shearers' quarters at Greentops Farm. Take a drink and keep walking to the top of a 300-metre peak above Greentops. Across the Oterei River lies Te Awaiti Station, the last 6400 hectares of Riddiford land and still the largest farm in the Wairarapa.

Chris and Jenny Bargh have farmed Greentops for nearly

The bushwalk on day three (left) is in marked contrast to the terrain encountered on day one (top right)—but it is all within the ability of the eager quartet setting out from the Little Tora Outstation (bottom).

TORA COASTAL WALK, SOUTH WAIRARAPA

TORA COASTAL WALK, SOUTH WAIRARAPA

TORA COASTAL WALK, SOUTH WAIRARAPA

30 years. It has been a good life, but in recent times Tora walkers have been almost as lucrative as sheep. That suits the couple because Jenny is passionate about cooking and Chris likes his fishing. The upshot is that Tora walkers get a beautiful seafood meal of fresh local cuisine and one they don't have to cook themselves. 'The best thing for me is when people leave here and say they are going to spread the word,' says Jenny Bargh. 'Most walkers are New Zealanders and they seem to like meeting people who are farming the land.'

The third, and final, day's walk, a four-and-a-half-hour return to the Outstation, is a 'river and bush' walk, first following the Oterei River before traversing an extensive block of native bush where more than 50 different species have been labelled. For a diversion, you can climb the Bugler, which at 255 metres ensures views as well as satisfaction, or pike out and keep on the trail to Little Tora. Either way, you should be back by 3 p.m.—having ticked the Tora off your tramping list.

Time Three days, three nights
Length 48 kilometres
Type Farm, bush, coastal
Start/finish Little Tora Outstation
Catering Fully catered
Pack carry Yes
Special features Food and views. Shuttle pick up available from Wellington airport.
Party number Up to 14
Accommodation Three fully-equipped lodges
Bedding Not supplied
Season 1 October to 30 April
Further information www.toracoastalwalk.co.nz

It may be a long way to see a rusting hulk but beach walking doesn't get much better than this.

Sheep, surf and wind-buttered hills are distinctive features of the Wairarapa Coast (pp. 116–117).

TORA COASTAL WALK, SOUTH WAIRARAPA 119

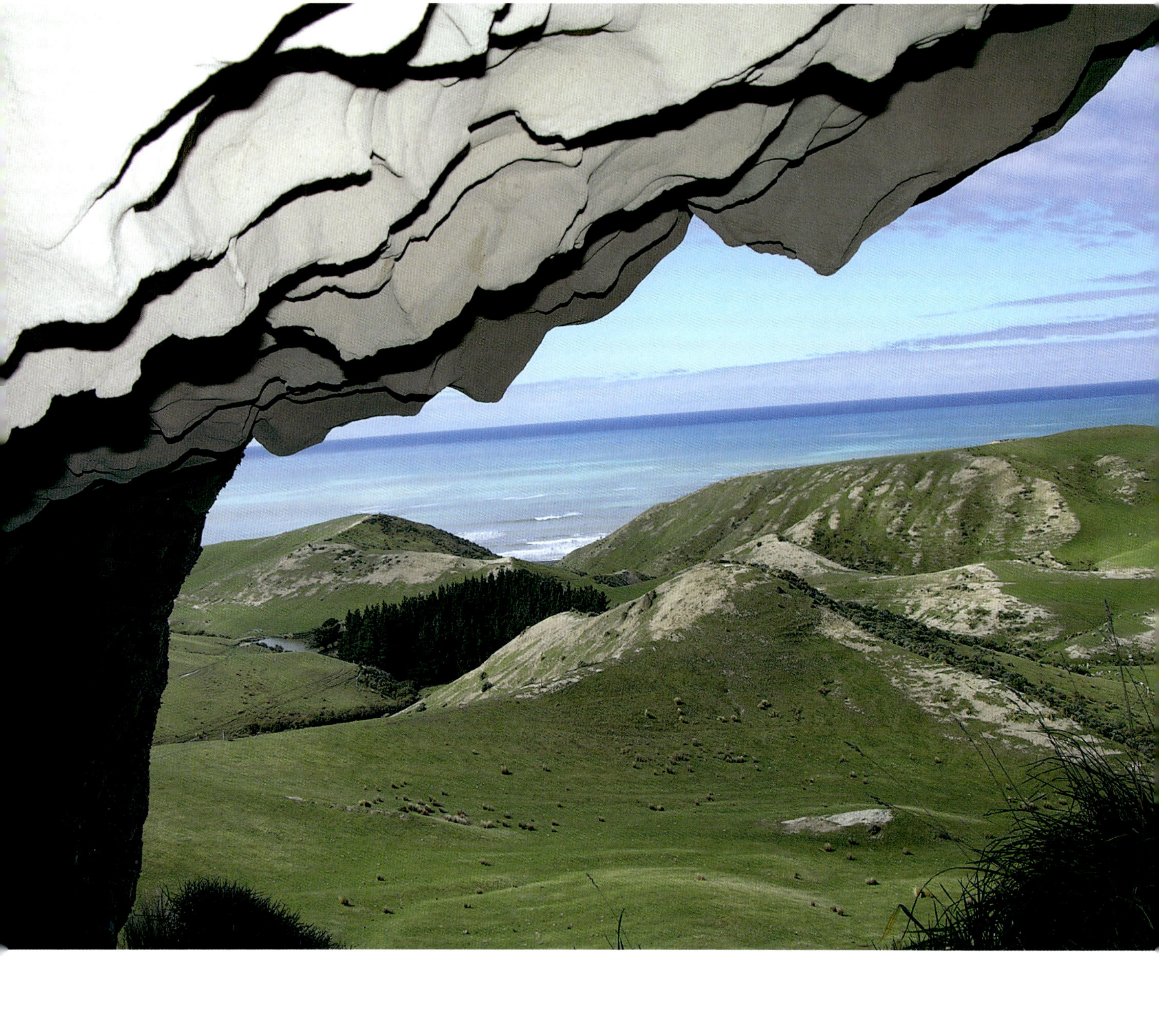

CAPTURED BY THE CAPE
CAPE CAMPBELL WALKWAY, WARD, MARLBOROUGH

There was a time when New Zealand trampers may have scoffed at the notion of trekking over farm pasture. Walking over grassy paddocks was something walkers in England did, not Kiwi trampers. But the advent of private trails in New Zealand, many of them routes over farmland, has caused many a hardened tramper to rethink and conclude that countryside walking can be as joyous as any rugged bush tramp.

Walking up hill and down dale over backcountry farms can be just as hard work—if hard work is what you are in the outdoors for—as tramping on many formed tracks in our National Parks. What is more, these are remote and uplifting areas of stunning scenery, places that encourage introspection and dreaming, and are surrounded by nature, albeit nature modified by man—in short, excellent tramping country. There is another feature of these trails that cannot be overstated: the landowners and the people who set up these walks are passionate about the country and its heritage. They are not just stocking their farms with people or selling a backcountry experience; they are sharing their family photograph album.

Nothing better illustrates this than the Cape Campbell Walkway, a four-day walk that traverses the coastline and fertile hills of two farms on the north-eastern tip of the South Island, between the Flaxbourne River and Lake Grassmere. Until 1905 the farms were part of the 30,500 hectare Flax-

Fierce winds whipping up from the Southern Ocean sculpt the Cape Campbell sandstone and erode the thin top soil.

bourne Station, established in 1847 by Sir Frederick Weld and Sir Charles Clifford. Maori lived near the coast at Clifford Bay, where the sea and the wetlands of the Grassmere estuary were a rich food basket. But the hills, flogged by almost constant winds from the south and in something of a rain shadow from the Inland Kaikoura Range, wore a spartan covering of tussock, tuahine scrub and stunted manuka. Still, Weld and Clifford stocked the property with thousands of sheep until the government bought the land under land-settlement legislation, cut it into blocks and put it up for ballot.

In one of those delightful instances of serendipity, Alfred Loe, a Christchurch stock agent and first generation New Zealander, got talking to a couple of fellow passengers on the train to the Waiau ewe sales. They had recently inspected the land at Flaxbourne and reckoned the homestead block was the best. When he got to Waiau, Alf telegrammed his father: 'Put in for the homestead block at Flaxbourne.' When he got home he was met by his father who signalled their success by throwing his hat in the air. The Loe family are still on the block—Kevin Loe is Alf's grandson—and have extended it with land from adjoining farms.

Next door is Cape Farm and the Freeth Estate, two other blocks in the Flaxbourne Station, both bought at auction in 1912 and farmed for years until they were bought by John Peter. The properties are now owned and farmed by his son Rob and wife, Sally. In farming families with such long pedigrees, each generation tends to introduce some new innovation. For neighbours Kevin and Carol Loe and Rob and Sally Peter, it was the creation, with considerable help from their families, of a 54 kilometre South Island trek over rugged hills in sight of the North Island and partly on a pack track used by isolated lighthouse keepers to fetch their supplies.

To ensure an early start, the first night of the walk is spent at Thorpelee Homestead, built in 1910 when ceiling studs catered for giants and wallpaper was exotic. In the paddocks around the house are the polo ponies that Kevin and Carol's sons breed and train for an international clientele, as well as riding professionally themselves. But if you get the chance, you should talk to Kevin Loe about his farming methods and his passion for the walkway. It is soon obvious that he sees the walkway as another way of 'farming' in harmony with the land. Loe, who as a young man worked on Molesworth Station as a horse breaker and head stockman, had a sort of farming epiphany a few years back in the aftermath of a typical Marlborough drought when he struggled to feed his stock.

The upshot was a decision to take stock to the feed rather than feed to the stock. Loe's sheep and cattle are now routinely sold off and trucked to drought-free areas, and the farm is restocked when the drought season is over. Loe has also fenced off a large paddock, given it a Queen Elizabeth II Trust covenant, and is allowing bush

Lunch shelters (top and bottom left) are fitted out for a hot brew of tea, coffee or soup. The Cape Campbell light (right) was first lit in 1870. The grounds include the grave of a lightkeeper's child (middle left) but the light has been unmanned since 1990.

CAPE CAMPBELL WALKWAY, MARLBOROUGH 123

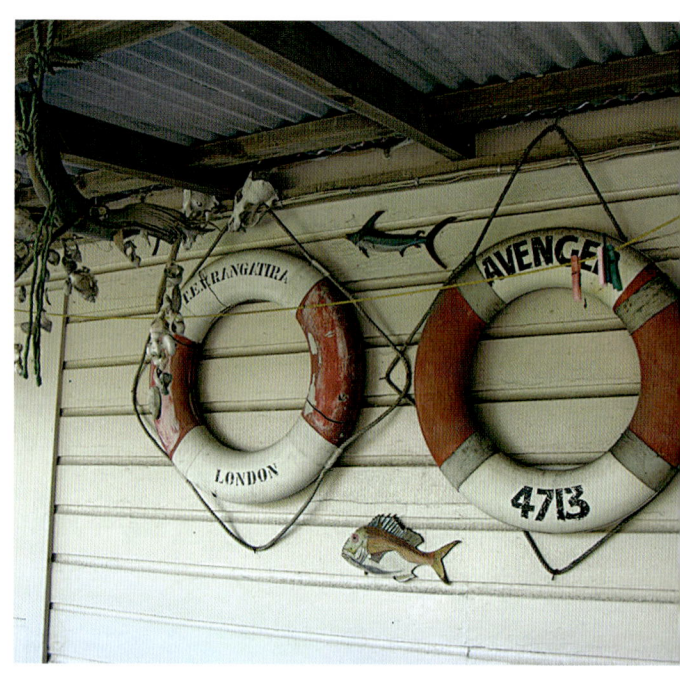

124　CAPE CAMPBELL WALKWAY, MARLBOROUGH

to regenerate. As part of his policy of working in harmony with the environmental peculiarities of his land, he has also declared peace with tuahine scrub and clumps of tussock. 'I noticed,' he says, 'that grass actually grew longest around the base of the scrub and that lambs hid among the tussock sheltering from the wind.' These are observations that Cape Campbell walkers can confirm.

Day one of the walk is a 17 kilometre trek that includes a climb to 350 metres where the Loes, with a touch of humour, have parked an old car in an otherwise vacant paddock facing the sea, with a sign that encourages lovers to cuddle up inside. On another high point is a strange cave where the prevailing southerlies have carved the sandstone ceiling into a delicately fluted texture. After your first day's walk you can relax and enjoy the comforts offered in The Shirt cottage, a quaint cottage set on a sunny hillside.

Much of the 12 kilometres of day two is spent hugging the rugged coastline that has claimed several ships. Low tide exposes extensive reefs rich in crayfish and paua. It's not jolly boating waters, but Rob Peter sets a cray pot by simply walking onto the reef at low tide. On the beach lie paua shells that are almost as big as a dinner plate.

The third evening of the walk is spent in the old 'single men's' quarters at the Cape Campbell lighthouse. The light, first lit in 1870, has been unmanned since 1990, and the two keepers' houses are gone. But the other buildings, now used by walkers, have been used as the Peters' family holiday home for many years, and photographs and the spoils of beachcombing bear testament to years of family fun. Seabirds and a couple of seals lounge on the reef below the 23 metre lighthouse, thoughtlessly repainted recently with two black bands rather than the traditional three shown in the walkway brochure and guide.

Day three, 10 kilometres long, climbs over Mt Tako (194 metres) and the remains of a Second World War radar station pointing across Cook Strait to the capital, and high, rolling hills of well-tended pasture with frolicking, bleating lambs, still wagging their tails behind them. To the north are Cape Terawhiti and Cape Palliser on the North Island, Kapiti Island and the hills of the Marlborough Sounds. To the south lies the unmistakable snow-covered summit of Mt Tapuae-o-Uenuku in the Inland Kaikouras. It stands on the horizon as you walk up a sweet limestone valley to the Freeth Estate House, built in Ward in 1908 as a boarding house, moved to its present site in 1946 and used in recent years as accommodation for farm staff.

With something of a magic touch, Sally Peter has transformed the house into a country cottage. Outside is an old-fashioned garden of paving stones and flowers. Inside is rich wooden flooring, a log fire, piano, super comfy beds, and an ambience that demands the occupants surrender

There is a touch of humour at a high point of the farm (top far left). Currents around the cape leave flotsam and jetsam which becomes appropriate adornment on the lighthouse accommodation (top right). New Zealand fur seals rest up on the rock platforms around the coast (above.)

First built as a boarding house in Ward, Freeth Cottage (bottom left) has been lovingly restored with a warm ambience indoors, cottage flower gardens and trellises made from manuka and old fence posts.

126 CAPE CAMPBELL WALKWAY, MARLBOROUGH

CAPE CAMPBELL WALKWAY, MARLBOROUGH

to relaxation. There is, it must be stressed, neither television nor cellphone reception.

The final day of 15 kilometres is across perhaps the most varied terrain—pasture, regenerating bush, patches of scrub and tussock, limestone outcrops, and small streams—before arriving back at Thorpelee. You should reach your vehicle by mid-afternoon and have plenty of time to travel south to Kaikoura and beyond, or north to Blenheim, Picton and an evening ferry crossing.

The most northerly stretch of the South Island's eastern coastline (pp. 126–127) can be fearsome and beguiling at the same time. (Above) The bare white cliffs on the long sweep of Cape Campbell catch the sun and sheep seeking a warm spot to rest.

Time Four days, four nights
Length 54 kilometres
Type Farmland, coastline
Start/finish Beach Rd, Ward, between Picton and Kaikoura
Catering Food available for purchase
Pack carry Yes
Special features Constantly changing landscape
Party number 10
Accommodation Fully equipped lodges, houses
Bedding Required
Season October to May
Further information www.capecampbellwalkway.co.nz

Cape
Campbell
Clifford Bay
Mussel Point
lighthouse
Lake Grassmere
shelter
Mt Tako
194m
Freeth
Estate
shelter
shelter
shelter
The Shirt Cottage
shelter
LIMESTONE RIDGE
London Hill
322m
Cave
shelter
Long Point
START/
FINISH
Thorpelee
to
Ward
Flaxbourne River
Chancet Rocks
North
Ward Beach

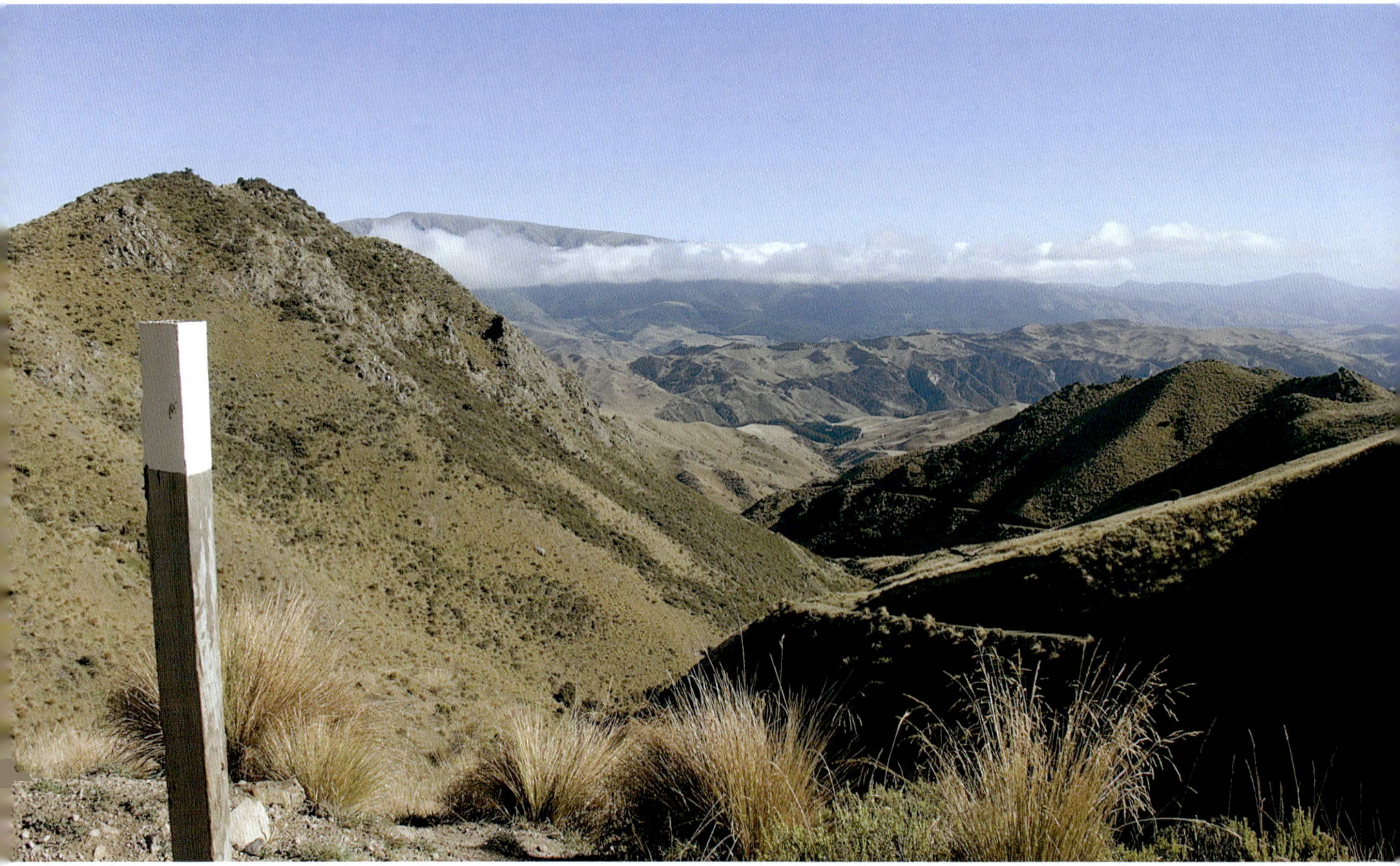

GOLDEN VINTAGE
AWATERE TUSSOCK TRACK, MARLBOROUGH

Unless you are a Marlborough local, you might have trouble getting directions to the Awatere Valley; the location that appears on the labels of some of New Zealand's best wines is not where you think it is. 'You mean the O-waatree,' the locals will eventually suggest, in determined defiance of correct Maori pronunciation.

However you say it, the valley, with its wide terraces left by an ancient river, is likely to become one of the best known in the country, at least to wine drinkers. For the area, where sheep and cattle once fattened on kilometre after kilometre of shingly terraces, has been given over to neat rows of grapevines. This has changed not only the farming in the district but the region too, as old Marlborough families now share their bounteous sunshine with migrant workers from the Pacific Islands, Asia and the Middle East, who come to pick and prune the grape crop.

Eventually, the valley narrows, the terraces shrink and the last few vineyards, before sheep and cattle return, look like a bit of a gamble. Follow the road past where the grapevines run out, and you will come to the legendary Molesworth Station—the country's largest farm with 180,000 hectares and 10,000 head of cattle, owned by the public to ensure that the high-country station, inland from Kaikoura, remains intact in perpetuity.

But throw a 'leftie' near the Awatere Bridge, where the Medway River joins the Awatere River, and before the road runs out you will come to Glen Orkney Station—1200 hectares of the Marlborough high country as it used to be. This is the location of the Awatere Tussock Track, a three-day walk contained within the boundaries of Glen Orkney that offers people the perfect way to see high-country farming up close.

There is something of a holistic feel to the walk, as owner Simon Harvey explains: 'We want the track and commercial farming to fit together as part of the whole visit.' So track walkers walk where Simon Harvey walks to do his shepherding and mustering; he uses neither horse nor farm bike.

Glen Orkney sits between the low country and the true high country, so walkers get a rare farming insight and expansive views of a landscape forever changing colour as the sun moves across a relentless azure sky. They can enjoy the sight of fine-fleeced Merino sheep grazing on pastures with the unkempt, golden clumps of native New Zealand tussock grass waving gently in the breeze. The farm is a long and narrow property with Mt Malvern at the head, the crags of Big Cregan, Little Cregan and Big Hill, all over 1000 metres, to the east, with the Blue Mountain Range beyond

Mid-point of day one on the Tussock Track and time to look across the Awatere Valley to the Black Birch Range

and the Medway River valley to the west. Far further to the west lies the imposing Black Birch Range.

Glen Orkney was formed in 1908 when a tough Scot from the Orkney Isles, J. W. Cummings, bought 1950 hectares of the former Welds Hill run, one of the pioneering nineteenth-century Marlborough pastoral properties. In 1938 Cummings divided the farm between his two sons, with Sinclair taking 750 hectares running along the Medway River to start the adjoining Stronsay Station, and his brother, Davy, taking the remainder of Glen Orkney. The brothers were a couple of hardy colonial boys with Davy using his experience as a sniper in the First World War to wage a relentless war on rabbits.

The western aspects of the snow-covered summit of Mt Tapuae-o-Uenuku in the Inland Kaikouras stamps its signature on the Marlborough high country.

He sold his hill and high-country tussock run to Denise and John Harvey in 1966. Cummings may have shot out most of the rabbits but little of the pasture had been fertilised, there were no farm roads and the only way to get around the station was to walk. But 20 years of hard work paid off for the Harveys in more ways than one. Their son, Simon, who with his wife, Lynda, took over the farm in 1985, is passionate about Glen Orkney. It is more than just their home and business; they are the custodians of a special piece of the New Zealand high country.

The land, which rises from 400 metres at the homestead to 1426 metres on the summit of Mt Malvern, is farmed quite conservatively, with 3200 Merino sheep and 150 Angus beef cattle. About half of the Glen Orkney income comes from beef and sheep meat; the other half comes from fine wool that is sold to make leisure and casual clothing. 'Merino are the best sheep for this country,' says Simon Harvey.' It is a neat fibre. I love everything about it. At shearing time when we are working with the wool it is so soft. It is a product I feel good about producing; you don't have to kill your animal to get it.'

There is an advantage in the way old man Cummings divided his land; it means that one man and his dogs can keep an eye on his flock by patrolling the centre of the station. It has another advantage too. This is tough land to farm with minimal rainfall and increasingly unpredictable dry periods. Flexible stock numbers and some innovation, such as crossing Merinos with polled Dorsets so as to produce a particularly lean and fine sheep carcass, may help with the economics but a bit of market research suggested the Harveys should add another dimension to the farm operation—people.

The nucleus was already there, thanks to Molesworth Station and a boutique Blenheim tourism company, The Molesworth Tour Company, that runs small group tours through Molesworth and the Marlborough high country. A feature of some of its tours was to stop at Glen Orkney for a fine farm lunch prepared by Lynda Harvey, complete with Awatere Valley wine and a chat from Simon on the legends and mysteries of high-country farming.

Some tours included an overnight stay at the stately Glen Orkney homestead, built by the Cummings in 1917 and beautifully maintained by Lynda Harvey, with a resplendent flower garden. The demands of the Awatere Track have since

One man and his dogs can manage a well-designed high-country station, where Merino flocks produce the finest wool to come off a sheep's back. Yarn spun from Merino fleece produces woollen fabric lighter than cotton.

put an end to the arrangement, but not before the Harveys had gained valuable hospitality experience. 'We realised that tourism was something that fitted in with what we were doing on the farm,' says Simon Harvey. 'We sort of bridge the gap between town and country; the people who come here are interested in the farming operation.'

Walkers who come to the Awatere Tussock Track will spend the first night in the Cummings' original home, built in 1910, later used as the shearers' quarters and most recently the first married home of Simon and Lynda Harvey.

The next day and you're heading off on an 8 kilometre walk of four to five hours along the eastern side of the farm, beneath the imposing heights of Big Hill and the rugged bluffs of Big Cregan. Look upwards and picture Simon Harvey and his dogs scampering up and down the tops, mustering sheep towards the trail you are following. You might also see an old trench hand dug by the Cummings for 3 kilometres to bring water to the homestead. It is a steady climb all day from the homestead at 400 metres to Cregan Hut at 650 metres, but there are many zigs and zags and ups and downs, including one over an 800 metre saddle. Along the way there are also three Queen Elizabeth II Trust covenanted areas that have been fenced off and where native plants are regenerating. The Harveys are dedicated conservationists and are past winners of the pastoral section of the Marlborough Environment Awards.

Retiring pockets of land for nature to reclaim fits with Simon Harvey's holistic approach to farming. Neighbouring Stronsay Station was recently on the market. It was tempting to reunite the original estate but, says Harvey laconically, the empire was likely to just get broken down again. Farming a smaller block may be a struggle in times when it seems to be drier, but there is a work–life balance to consider. 'I have been here since I was four years old,' he says. 'We could have gone for a bigger farm but I want to make this farm as good as we can. We will fence off some

The Glen Orkney homestead was built in 1917 and its magnificent flower gardens have been faithfully maintained by Lynda Harvey. In spring and summer the flower beds, most with antique varieties, are a riot of colour.

AWATERE TUSSOCK TRACK, MARLBOROUGH 135

AWATERE TUSSOCK TRACK, MARLBOROUGH

AWATERE TUSSOCK TRACK, MARLBOROUGH

bits, improve others and give walkers a contrast. The drier weather may be tough for farming but it is good for walkers because most days are fine.'

The second night is spent in Cregan Hut, purpose-built by the Harveys but in a style quite fitting to an outback walk. It includes some nice touches with rough-hewn timber created by their apprentice-carpenter son.

Day two on the Tussock Track is a bit of a toughie—it's just 5 kilometres long but likely to take you up to six hours. It is a loop from Cregan Hut towards Mt Malvern that passes through a few patches of Hall's totara that escaped the forest burning of Maori moa hunters, climbing to Twin Peaks at 1200 metres. Beyond Billy Goat Saddle under the rocky northern face of Mt Malvern, there is a musterers' hut that gives shelter and shade for lunch.

After another night at Cregan Hut, you're into the final day's walk, which follows the station's western boundary to return you to the Glen Orkney homestead. While the terrain is similar to day one, both the track and views are quite different. Along the way it passes, beside a small creek, an old musterers' hut that has been fitted out as a museum of the station's early days. It tells the tale of Simon's father,

John Harvey, being marooned there while the creek was in flood, until his ageing neighbour, Sinclair Cumming, rode his old horse through the flooded creek to bring his young neighbour home to a worried family.

These days there should be no such dramatic experiences on the track, but you will leave with great memories from this very special piece of New Zealand.

Mt Malvern (pp. 136–137) dominates the southern view of the Awatere Tussock Track. The twin rocky peaks at the right are reached on day two and are the highest point on the track. The walk back to the Glen Orkney homestead (above) follows the station's western boundary.

An old musterers' hut (top left) has been turned into a museum that tells the tale of high-country farming a century ago. Cregan Hut (bottom right) has the luxury of solar-powered electricity.

Time Three nights, three days
Length 22 kilometres
Type Farmland, subalpine tussock
Start/finish Glen Orkney Station homestead, Awatere valley
Catering No
Pack carry Yes
Special features Microcosm of the Marlborough high country
Party number 8
Accommodation Fully featured cottages
Bedding Not provided
Season Mid November to mid May
Further information www.tussocktrack.co.nz

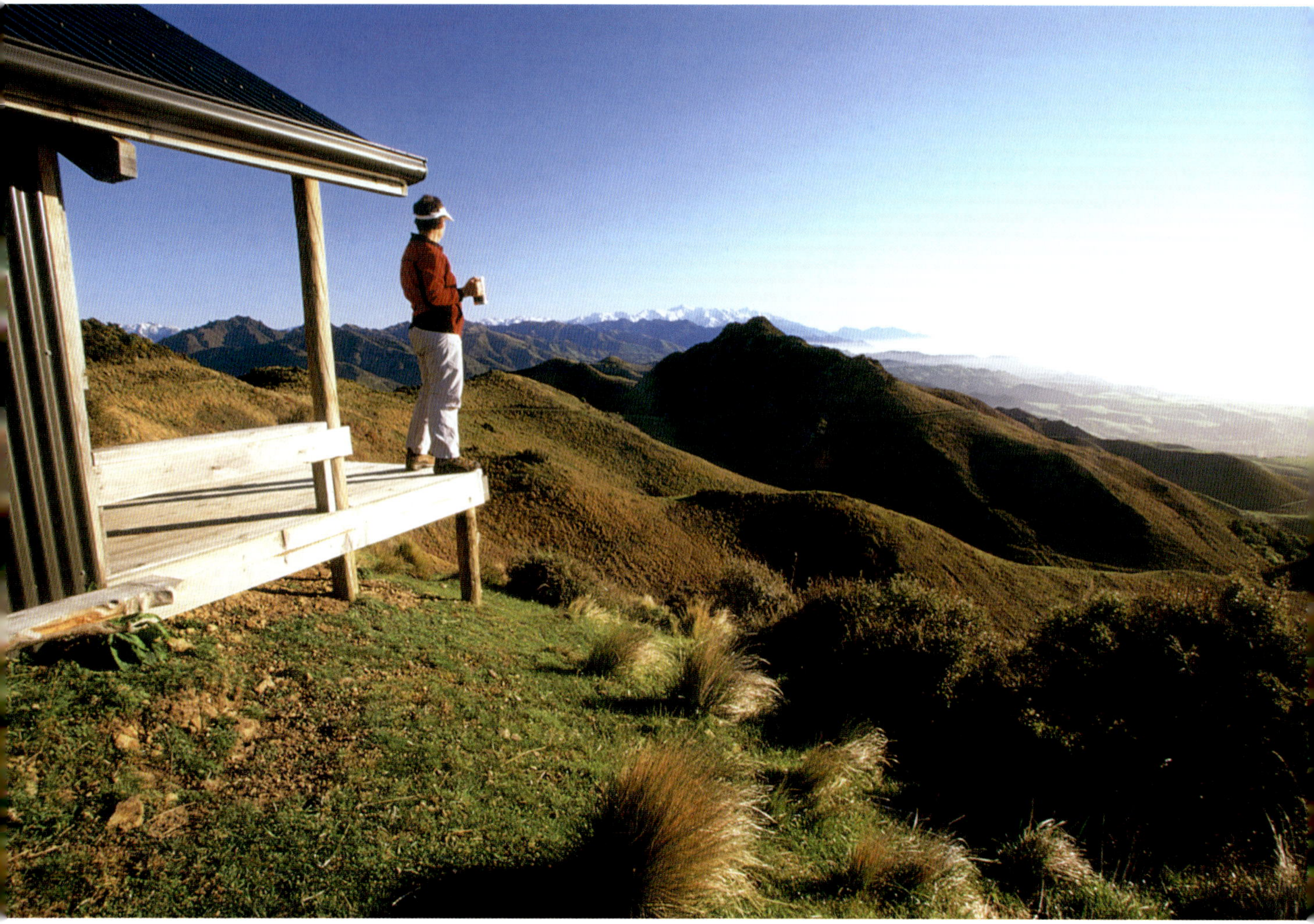

WHALE OF A WALK
KAIKOURA COAST TRACK, NORTH CANTERBURY

The Kaikoura Coast Track is just about as well known as the whales that play off the coast a few kilometres to the north. While many thousands of tourists go whale-watching, seasoned trampers head for the track, the second private walk to be established in New Zealand.

Walkers might not spot a whale, but they may, if they are lucky, see Hector's or Dusky dolphins at play in the surf, or a seal taking a siesta on the beach.

But they will almost certainly get to share a story or two with fellow trampers. With its relative proximity to Christchurch and straightforward loop structure, the Kaikoura Coast Track, 50 kilometres south of Kaikoura, has marked itself as a favoured adventure for those who have no intention of hanging up their boots just because their rucksack is beginning to feel a tad heavy, or for fitness groups keen to step out on something other than urban footpaths. Such walkers generally like to ramble in the company of familiar outdoor companions and chatter away about trips shared in the past as well as the delights of the trail they are following.

On the three-day Kaikoura Coast circuit around three farms, there are plenty of opportunities to yarn while you stop and admire a stunning view, or pause for a little solitude as the sun settles on the distant snow-topped peaks of the Inland and Seaward Kaikoura mountains.

The magnificent sweep of the Kaikoura coast against a backdrop of snow-covered ranges is the constant visual feature of the Kaikoura Coast Track.

Early or late in the season there may even be a light dusting of snow on the 600 metre tops of the Hawkswood Range to add a romantic touch to the adventure.

With its mix of farm roads, rolling pastureland, enclaves of native bush and long stretch of wild coastline, the Kaikoura Coast Track has become the benchmark and model for many other private treks.

The trail begins 140 kilometres north of Christchurch, just off SH1 at the Staging Post, once the nerve centre of the Hawkswood property that used to encompass 23,000 hectares of coastal land between the Conway and Waiau Rivers, including the entire route of the Kaikoura Coast Track. In the 1860s Hawkswood was famous for its hospitality, its orchard and its cider. Many travellers rested the night on a journey along the coast, and there was always station fare of mutton and vegetables.

It is too complicated to detail here the many intricacies of how the estate has been split up, who has farmed what, married whom and fathered whom since farming began in 1859. But if you are curious to find out more about the estate, now 1820 hectares, you can always visit the Hawkswood museum and archive of the family's military record. It was established by the renowned Hawkswood patriarch,

J. D. Macfarlane, in one of the houses his ancestors built in the nineteenth century.

It was also the delightfully eccentric J. D. who established the Staging Post as a tourist destination in 1982, when he invited the Southern Ballet and various other artists to appear over a two-day outdoor festival at Hawkswood. The endeavour was so successful that the large outdoor stage on which the artists performed has since been used for a wide variety of functions, and the Hawkswood homestead, somewhat in the manner of the 1860s, has become an odd assortment of backpackers' accommodation, rustic bunkhouses of unsawn logs or mud bricks, campground, farmstay, farm walks, functions and wedding venue. An old implement shed houses J. D.'s collection of horse-drawn vehicles, old farm machinery, and a blacksmith's forge that looks just as it must have done nearly 150 years ago.

Among the collection of buildings is Ash House, built primarily to accommodate the Kaikoura Coast Track walkers on their first night. The next day it's time to begin the walk, after being bussed to the starting point at Buntings Bush, nine kilometres north on SH1. The destination is 13 kilometres over the Hawkswood Range to Ngaroma Homestead on the coast, the farm of Bruce and Heather Macfarlane, a distant relation of J. D.

The Hawkswood Range reaches to 600 metres but the gradient, initially through a 120 hectare pine plantation, is gentle. Buntings Bush is a remnant of an old beech forest, of which there are few now left in Canterbury. Since 2002 some 135 hectares of it has been fenced off from farm animals and protected under a Queen Elizabeth II Trust covenant. The beech gives way to giant podocarps such as kahikatea, matai and totara, and a couple of conveniently placed seats—one signposted Heather's Seat, the other Bruce's Seat—offer both a rest and views across to the usually snow-covered Inland Kaikouras.

Beyond lies Skull Peak and a panoramic view north and south of the Kaikoura coast, with the Pacific Ocean surf almost crashing at your feet. The high peaks of the Seaward Kaikouras—Manakau (2610 metres), Uwerau (2227 metres) and Te Ao Whekere (2596 metres)—rise above the Kaikoura Peninsula running out into the Pacific Ocean. A little way below the lookout is Skull Peak Shelter, where you can brew up a cuppa or enjoy some lunch. As a stopping point, it doesn't come much better than this—the view of a narrow green strip of pasture and the coast at your feet is magnetic.

The track into Ngaroma and the night's accommodation at Ngaroma Loft, a purpose-built trekkers' bunkhouse within sight and sound of the ocean, is through another

The Staging Post has welcomed visitors for nearly 150 years. A family museum and a collection of old vehicles and farm machinery are reminders of the days when the farm covered 23,000 hectares of the Kaikoura coast.

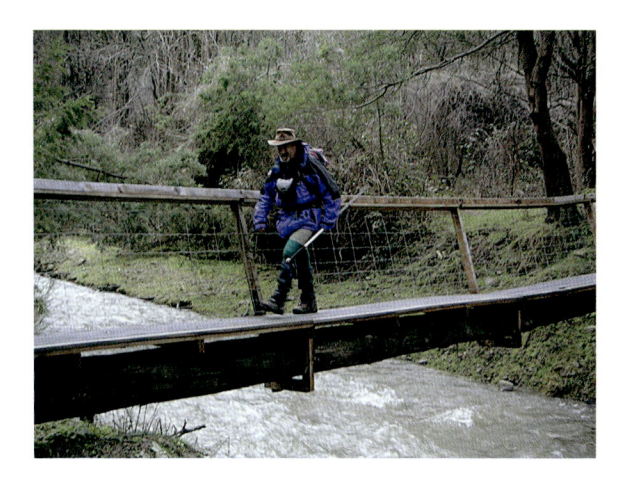

KAIKOURA COAST TRACK, NORTH CANTERBURY 143

fenced-off block of bush where many of the trees have been thoughtfully labelled. A century ago the warmer coastal climes of Ngaroma were used as lambing pastures for the Hawkswood station.

Day two of about 13 kilometres is a dawdle day, most of it at sea level, and all of it a quite fascinating study in geology and the changes wrought on the land by glaciations and fault movements during the last 14,000 years. Past Sawpit Creek, the beach and cliff face are embedded with tree trunks from an 8000-year-old forest of matai, rimu and kanuka that was buried and preserved in sediment until coastal erosion exposed their corpses. There are fossil shell traces on the cliffs and patterns lefts by layers of glacial flour,

Sometimes the coast is spectacularly wild—and sometimes dolphins and seals can be seen playing in the surf.

blown out to sea from the inland mountains and washed up on shore. It is not unusual to see Hector's or Dusky dolphins, or seals at play in the surf, while at your feet are colourful pebbles that have been polished by the surf.

If you fancy a brew-up for lunch, collect some driftwood because at Circle Shelter, where the trail leaves the beach, you'll find a billy, paper, matches and tea. After lunch you climb onto the coastal pastures of Medina, farmed by Sally and David Handyside in partnership with their son Peter and his wife, Megan. A feature of Medina is the extensive

KAIKOURA COAST TRACK, NORTH CANTERBURY 145

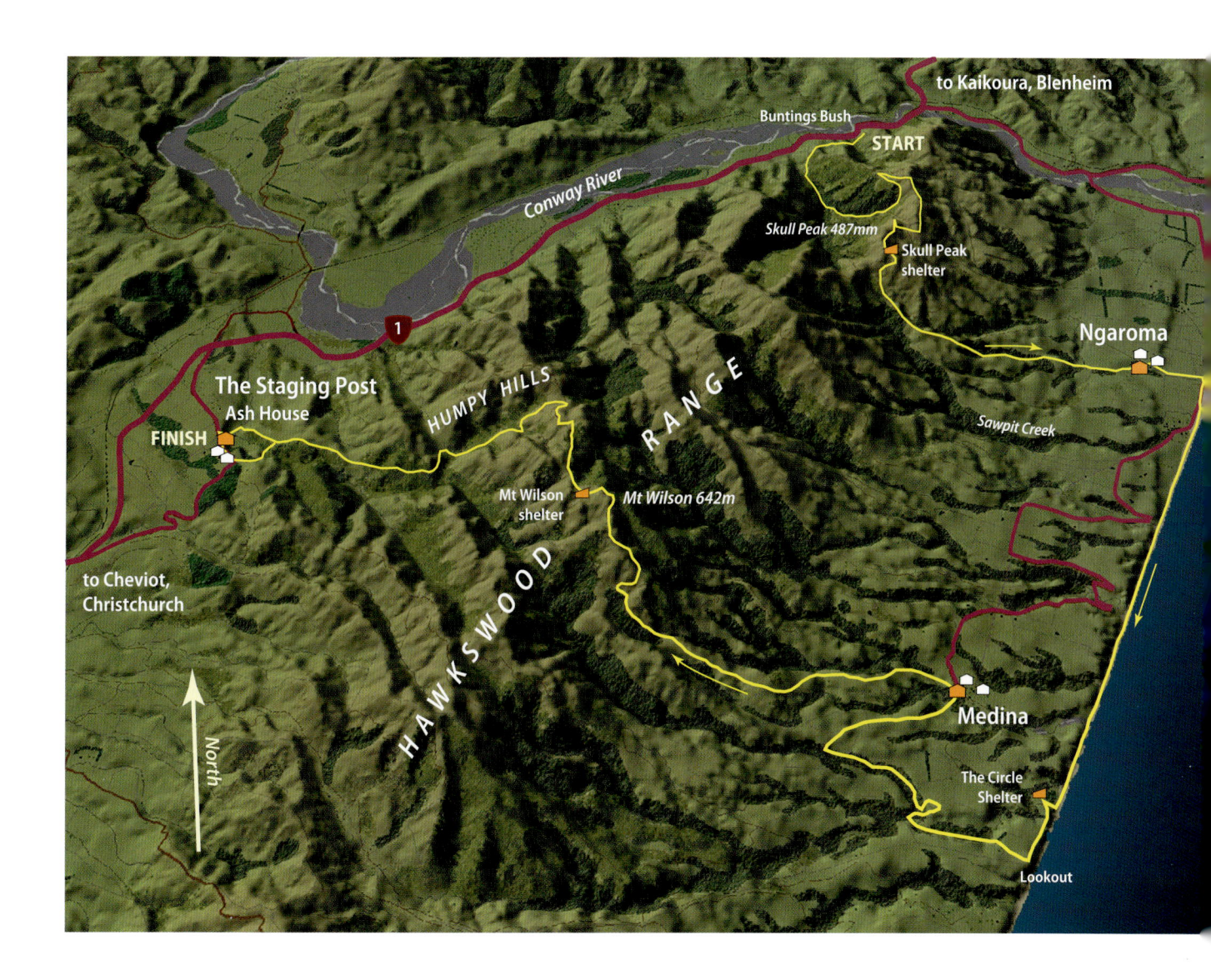

146 KAIKOURA COAST TRACK, NORTH CANTERBURY

KAIKOURA COAST TRACK, NORTH CANTERBURY

gullies that the Handysides have fenced off since 1982 and are now thick with regenerating native bush, including some grand old matai and kahikatea, and birdlife. The trail wanders through the gullies and across streams for a couple of hours, to add another distinctive element to the track.

One of the real delights of these walks is the time spent with your hosts; disdain self-catering and instead dine on roast lamb and a sumptuous array of vegetables, and talk into the night about farming, children, other treks and adventure travel overseas. There is no need to feel guilty about taking up your hosts' time; meeting people is one of the reasons why farmers such as the Macfarlanes and Handysides set up these walks.

Day three is another 13 kilometres back over the Hawkswood Range to the Staging Post. A small detour to the summit of 642 metre Mt Wilson provides a 360-degree view over the Culverden Basin to the Inland Kaikoura Range. A little further on at the Mt Wilson Shelter and suggested lunch spot, there is a wonderful view of a distant Mt Tapuae-o-Uenuku, the highest peak in the South Island outside of the Southern Alps, and a fitting image to carry from the Kaikoura coast.

A novel sign on a toilet door (above) is a typical piece of rural humour found on a walking track devised by farmers.

The spectacular scenery of the Seaward Kaikouras (top right) and as seen from the Skull Peak Shelter (bottom right) are the mark of the Kaikoura Coast Track.

The track crosses the Hawkswood Range (pp. 146–147) from west to east and from east to west.

Time Three days, three nights
Length 40 kilometres
Type Farm, bush and coastal
Start/finish The Staging Post, Hawkswood
Catering On request
Pack carry Yes
Special features Stunning coastal views
Party number Up to 10
Accommodation Three fully equipped lodges
Bedding Not supplied
Season October to April inclusive
Further information www.kaikouratrack.co.nz

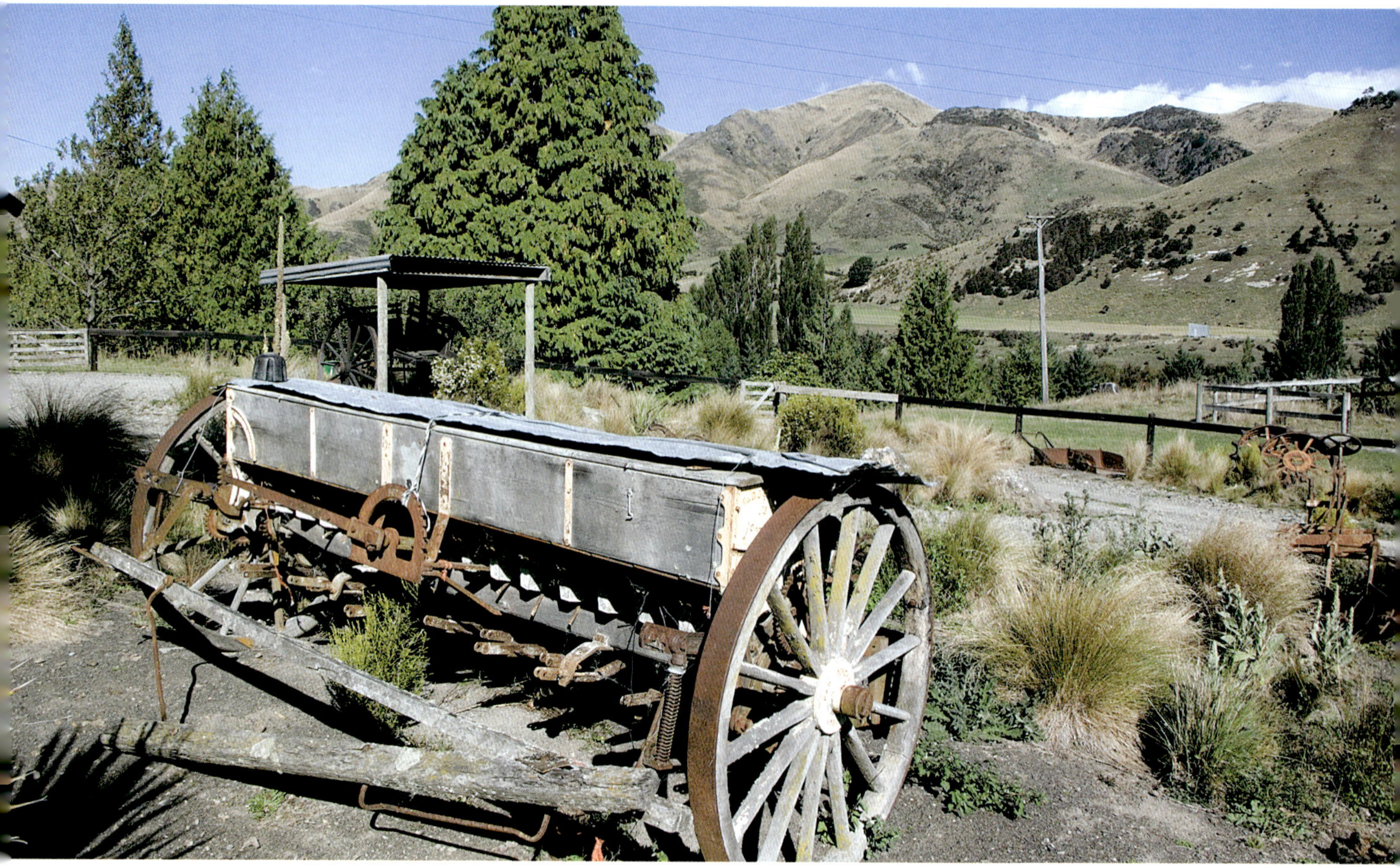

HOME, SWEET HOME
HURUNUI HIGH COUNTRY TRACK, HURUNUI, NORTH CANTERBURY

Dan Shand is hardly your stereotype prodigal son—having spent his youth on the family high-country station, most of the time with his sleeves rolled up, he dutifully did a university degree before heading off overseas on the young Kiwis' rite of passage, the big OE.

If there was a blip anywhere it was only that the young Shand, fourth generation to farm the 7100 hectare station of Island Hills in North Canterbury, took his degree in marketing and design rather than in anything agricultural.

'You have to have a good reason to come home,' says Dan, now looking very much the epitome of a windburnt hill farmer. And in Australia he found one—Mandy, twin sister of his flatmate. They had met before in school and university days in the way that Canterbury farming children seem to. Now the Waimate farmer's daughter was working on the Queensland coast as a scuba-diving instructor, which is about as different a career to high-country farming that you can get—with the exception, perhaps, of Dan's career choice of website designer.

They fell in love, dreamed of a perfect future, got married and turned their dreams into the reality of the Hurunui High Country Track. Running a private walking track seemed to be the perfect way to use their people skills and love of

The pioneering past is a fascinating feature on walks such as the Hurunui High Country Track, leaving a visual reminder of those who walked the land for their livelihood.

the outdoors in an environment they were both passionate about—the North Canterbury high country. The couple's education and practical farming background, along with Dan's intimate knowledge of the terrain and history of the Island Hills Station, gave them just the right synergy to create and develop a distinctive private walk and produce marketing and business plans.

They studied other similar walking operations to see what they thought worked and what didn't, and where they might be able to add something distinctive to their own operation. They were fortunate, says Dan, in that the nucleus of the accommodation was already there.

'Without having the accommodation already in place we could never have done this,' he says. But first came 12 months of backbreaking work setting up the track to a standard the couple was happy with, while they survived on a meagre income from a few freelance website design commissions and selling possum skins and fur. 'I reckon we lived on about $4000 the first year we were home,' says Dan. 'If we hadn't been living on a farm we could never have done it.' And, with Dan's father semi-retired, farming a 200 hectare fattening unit at Balmoral, there was still a station, carrying 3000 stock units—sheep, cattle and deer—to run.

The track opened in a modest way in 2003 and there have been many improvements made since. The farming side of Island Hills is now run as a partnership with another family, leaving the Shands more time to concentrate on the Hurunui Track and develop a bee-keeping business that produces premium manuka honey. It's a perfect combination. A century ago, when shepherds were paid barely a dollar a week, the hills of Island Hills Station were mostly in tussock, farmers continued the regular burn-offs first started

You can cross Bush Creek (above) without getting your feet wet to reach Bush Hut (top right).

by Maori moa-hunters, and far more stock were carried on fenceless properties cared for by a team of shepherds and boundary riders.

But the economics have changed; the return from sheep on marginal land doesn't justify the cost of looking after them so the land has been retired from grazing. That is good news for walkers and wildlife because, somewhat surprisingly, it is regenerating in bush that no one in living memory has seen, and at lower levels in thick manuka. The Shands now have more than 400 hives producing pure manuka honey, and looking after them fits in with the daily pack run and tidying and cleaning the huts. In a block of native bush retired under Queen Elizabeth II Trust covenant, some 44 native species have been labelled alongside the track.

Perhaps it is because of their age or their background, but little touches added by Dan and Mandy tend to set the Hurunui Track apart. It starts at the former shearers' quarters at the Island Hills Station, where guests spend a night before beginning the first day's walk. Built in 1914, the quarters have been renovated into a comfortably appointed lodge, but what may strike you most is the ringing of the old-fashioned telephone on the wall. It will be Mandy or Dan calling from their home close by to announce they will be over in five minutes for a trip briefing. Any telephone could have been used, but Dan and Mandy's novel choice to wire up the old phone already there sets the scene for a walk that already differs from your average National Park tramp.

The first day is a long but mainly easy walk over 14.6 kilometres, a good half of which is along the Glencoe River. It takes it name from the Glencoe valley in Scotland where the MacDonalds were massacred, and here in New Zealand there was a similar slaughter, but this time sheep, after an early run-holder was forced to slaughter his whole mob of 6000 scab disease-ridden animals. It was said the river ran red all the way to Hurunui.

In the cliffs on the other side of the river are signs of an extinct volcano and seabed fossils left behind by an ancient sea that once stretched across the Canterbury Plains. A forest of Douglas-fir is the interesting legacy of a New Zealand Forest Service experiment in the late 1960s. Every second

Accommodation for visiting shearing gangs and huts for shepherds were once essential on every large station. Shearers and shepherds are now more mobile and the disused buildings are used to good effect to house track walkers.

Wonderfully cool, pure water tumbles out of the high country down Bush Creek. Quenching your thirst is irresistible.

row was planted in *Pinus contorta* under the theory that the *contorta* would force the Douglas-fir to grow up with few branches until it blocked the light and the *contorta* died off, thus saving pruning. In places it looks to have worked but *contorta* is such a vociferous wilding species that the experiment is unlikely to be repeated.

High point of the day is at 750 metres, from where there are views to Lake Sumner Forest Park, which adjoins Island Hills, and past the Lewis Pass road to Mt St Andrew. One of the features of the Hurunui Track is the thoughtful little things provided. Just when you feel like a cuppa you come across a small table in the wilderness with a bag containing some afternoon tea goodies and a couple of Thermoses of hot water. And waiting in the fridge at the Valley Camp Hut, perhaps, a bottle of sparkling wine to celebrate your arrival. It is why, when Dan comes to clean the next day, he is liable to find pinned to the wall a note reading: 'Dear Mandy and Dan, What a lovely surprise! Many thanks. It's the little things that count and you are both so good at it.'

The large open-plan hut at Valley Camp sits among beech trees where bellbirds welcome your arrival, while the sun throws shadows on the surrounding high peaks. A musterers' hut has been on the idyllic site since 1933 but the present hut owes its existence to a deer poacher. Caught using the old hut as a hunting base without permission, he ended up becoming a lifelong friend of the Shands, and he and his mates built the spacious new hut initially for hunting. Dan has now equipped it with solar-powered lighting, a refrigerator and a gas caliphont hot shower. It also has a radio so you can let Dan and Mandy know all is well. The Mandamus River bubbles along just by the hut, and a typical entry in the visitors' book reads: 'What a beautiful spot. We threw ourselves into the river and later enjoyed a long hot shower. Bliss!'

Day two is over rougher terrain but it is shorter at 8.2 kilometres and includes delightful sections of broadleaf, and beech forest when the vegetation changes to subalpine. The birdlife is varied and abundant, relishing the Shands' ongoing war on pests such as stoats and rats.

Accommodation for the night is in Bush Hut, which sits in a small clearing in the beech forest. Backcountry huts don't

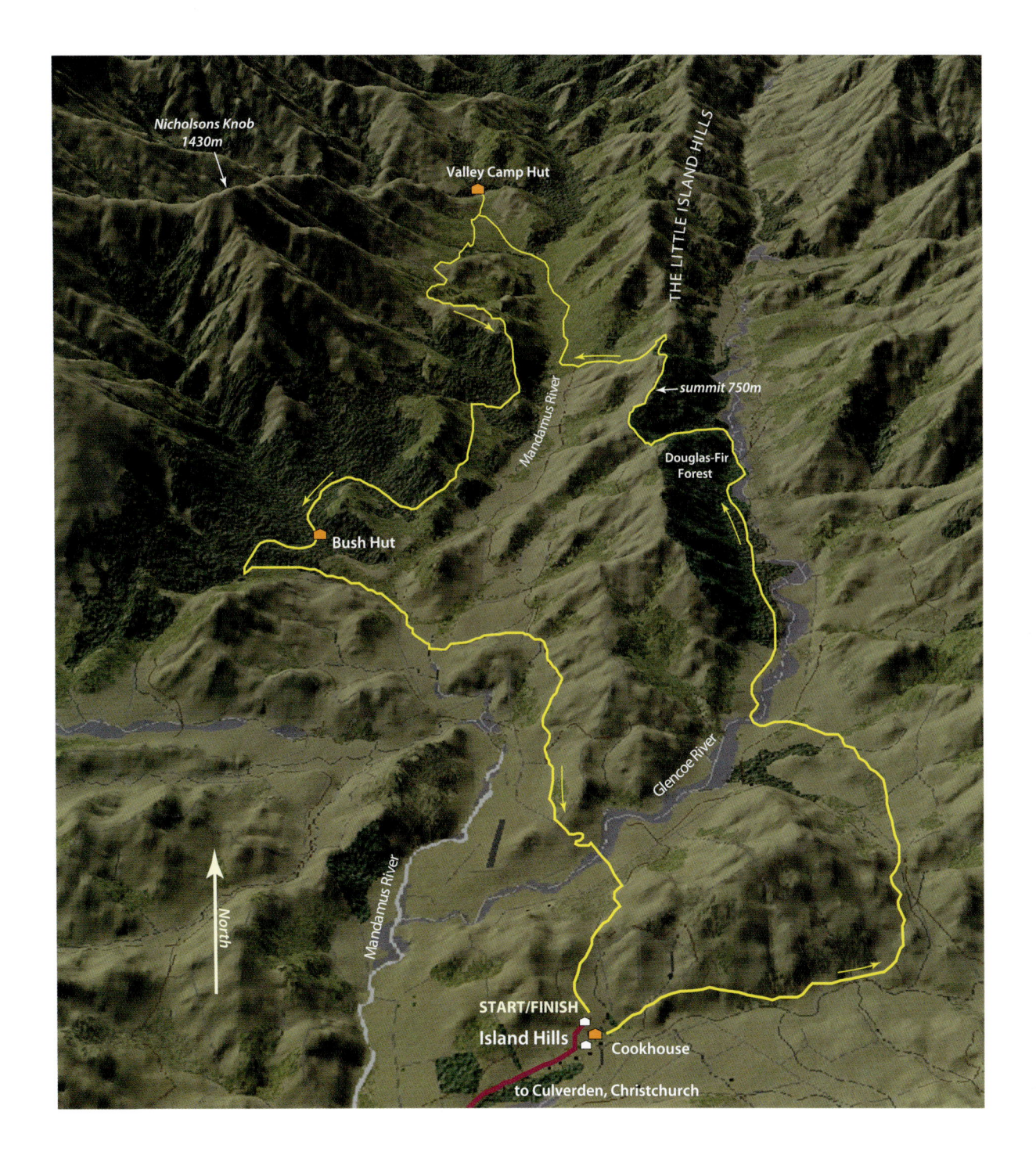

HURUNUI HIGH COUNTRY TRACK, HURUNUI, NORTH CANTERBURY

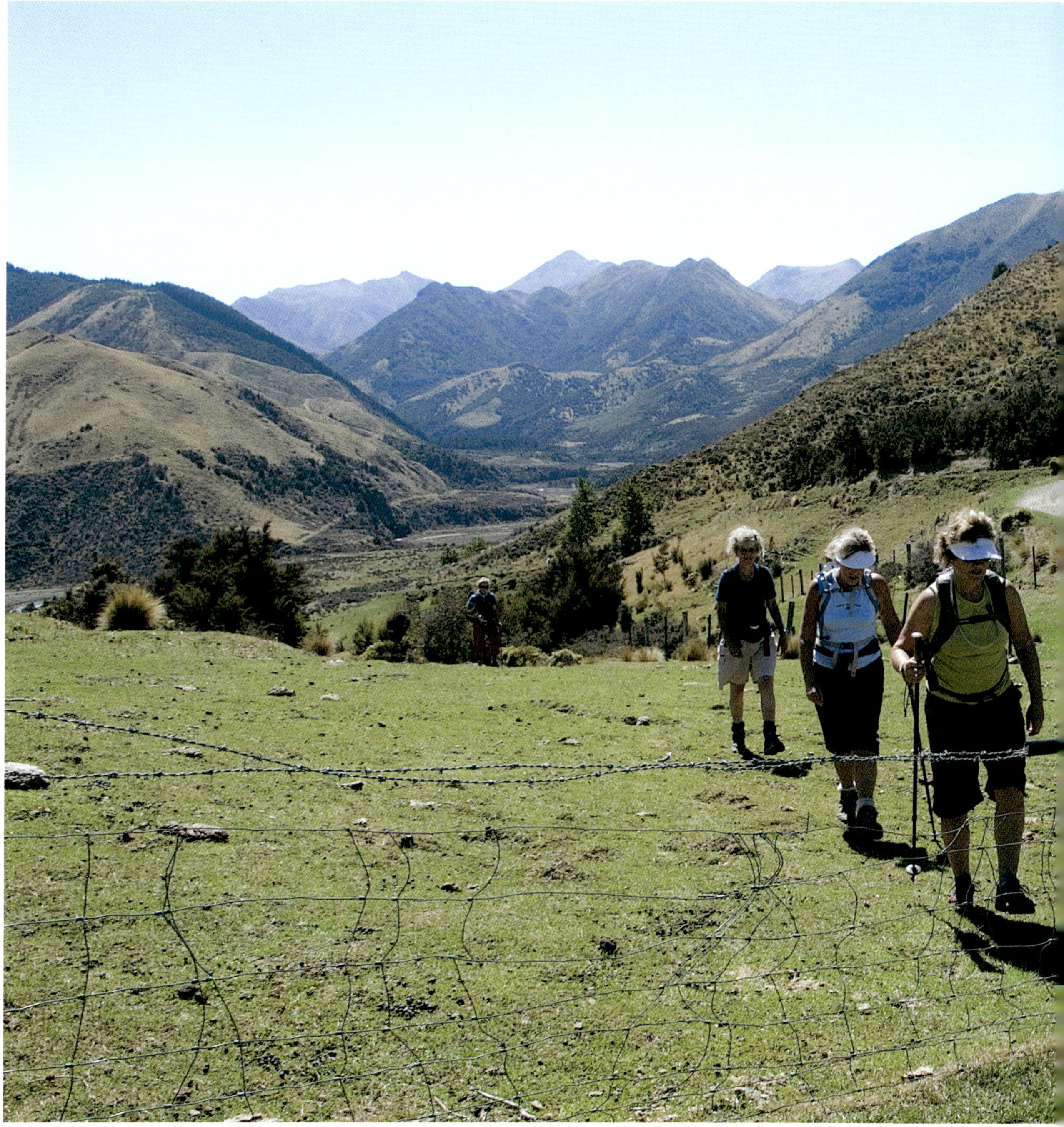

HURUNUI HIGH COUNTRY TRACK, HURUNUI, NORTH CANTERBURY 157

come more appealing than this red beech log cabin built in the Depression by a Norwegian craftsman, Chris Johnson. Shepherds who have used the hut include double VC war hero Charles Upham, head shepherd at Island Hills from 1934 to 1936—but they never had the luxury enjoyed by today's walkers of hot showers and gas cookers.

The final day is 7 kilometres of mainly easy walking through native bush and over high-country farmland. It is just what most walkers order because a night in Bush Hut tends to bring out the party spirit—particularly when there is someone else to carry the wine. Most groups arrive back at the cookhouse by early afternoon, leaving plenty of time to set out on the journey home. Before you leave you should make a point of visiting the small museum of farm memorabilia that the Shands have set up. Some of it has been unearthed from their own home which was built in 1882 for Angus McLoud, head shepherd for the giant 16,000 hectares Glens of Tekoa Station from which 7100 hectares was split off as Island Hills and sold to Dan's great-grandfather in 1928.

An interesting museum with farm memorabilia has been set up by Dan and Mandy Shand (top right)

Time Three days, three nights
Length 30 kilometres
Type Bush, farmland, subalpine
Start/finish Island Hills Station
Catering No
Pack carry Yes
Special features Varied scenery, wildlife, comfort in the wilds
Party number Eight to 10
Accommodation Three fully featured huts and lodge
Bedding Not supplied
Season November to April
Further information www.walkingtrack.co.nz

The sons managed the station and Dan's grandparents lived in the farm-baked brick cottage all their lives. When Dan and Mandy moved into the almost derelict cottage they discovered that grandma never threw anything out and the results of her hoarding make fascinating viewing in the tiny museum.

Where the bush has been left to regenerate it is soon thick with native birds such as the kereru (wood pigeon) (above).

(Pp. 156–157) Journey's end—a group of Hurunui Track walkers are just one stile away from the end of a three-day high-country trek.

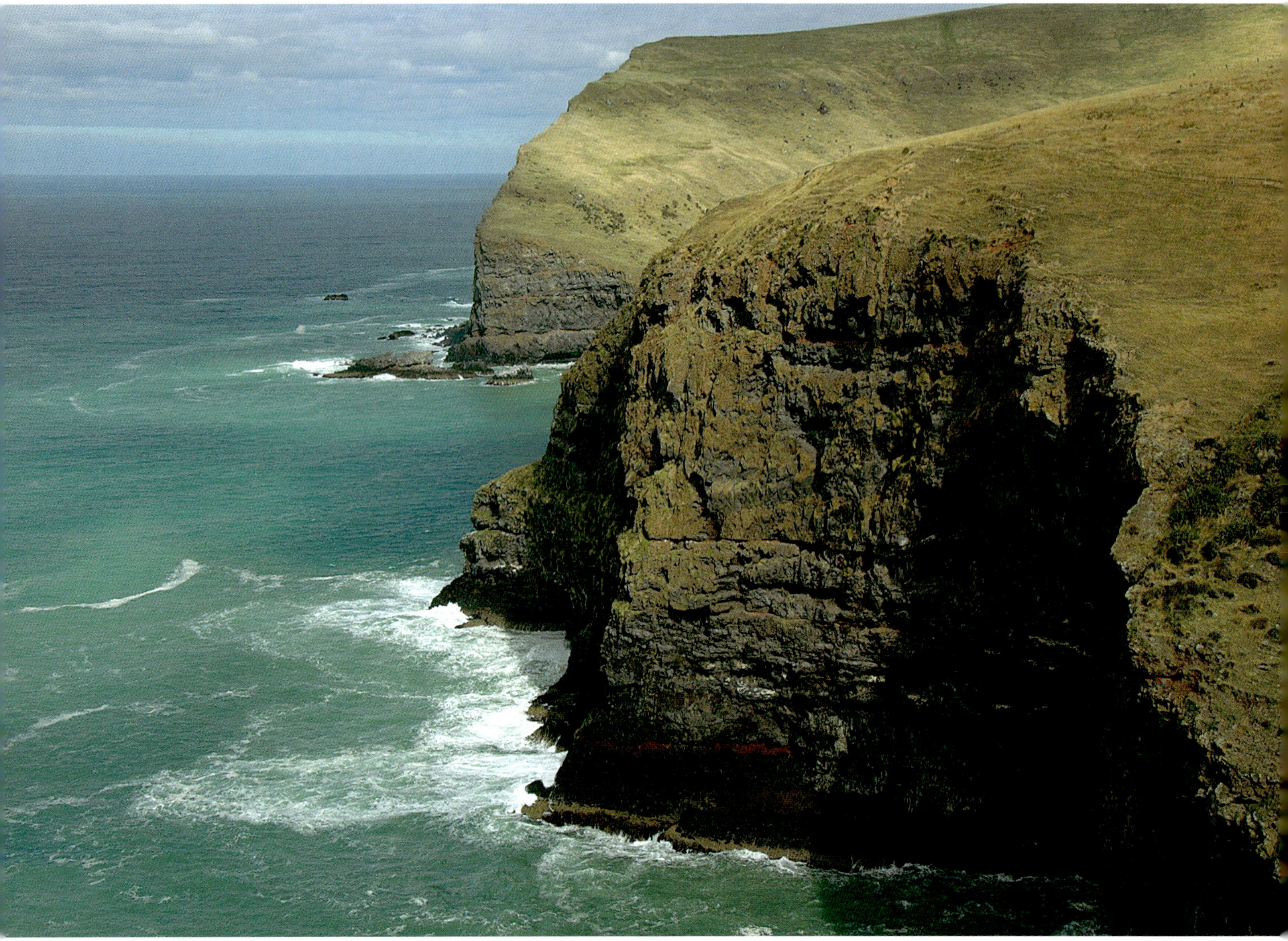

IN THE BEGINNING
BANKS PENINSULA TRACK, AKAROA, CANTERBURY

Farmers the world over love to moan about everything, from the government to the weather. In New Zealand, back in the mid-1980s, farmers had more cause than usual. A reforming Labour government was taking a wrecking ball to fortress New Zealand, and farming, the traditional backbone of the economy, was not left unscathed.

Under the new levelled playing field, a plethora of tax breaks, development incentives, fertiliser and other subsidies, and an abundance of free advice that farmers had enjoyed for years to keep New Zealand agriculture competitive with the obscenely subsidised and market-protected farmers of Europe and elsewhere disappeared. It was amid this climate that a group of farmers from Banks Peninsula, near Christchurch, were having a chinwag at a party on how they could make their farms viable in the face of a bad drought and Rogernomics paddock-flattening. During the chat someone came up with the revolutionary idea of charging people to walk over their farms.

That was May 1989. By December the first customers, most of them solicited from the backpacker hostels of Akaroa, were walking the Banks Peninsula Track. 'We were the first and we're the best,' says Steve Helps, one of the eight partners in the operation, proudly. In the first year 296 people walked the track. Now it attracts about 2600 walkers a year. 'We feel we are the leaders in the private walks circuit and we try to keep our standards high and keep ahead of the pack,' says Helps.

The private track idea had considerable traction from the beginning. Akaroa, with its intriguing French heritage, is one of the country's most charming and deliciously sited tourist towns. It is a natural magnet for visitors young and old, has a wide variety of accommodation and is easily reached by public transport from Christchurch, 85 kilometres away. It is, in short, an ideal place to begin and end a four-day walk.

The track partners' farmland includes significant native bush remnants, stunning coastal scenery, wildlife havens for penguins and seals, plus some farm buildings surplus to requirements—just the place for a 35 kilometre hike of 'four nights, four days, four beaches, four bays.' And perhaps of most import to the track's ongoing success is that the partners, like farmers everywhere, are individualists, so each day of the walk has its own distinct characteristics, quite apart from the changes in the terrain.

The walk begins with a pickup in Akaroa in late afternoon and a shuttle to the Hamilton family homestead on a magnificent 400 hectare sheep spread at Onuku, overlooking

Soaring basalt cliffs tell of the volcanic origins of Banks Peninsula.

Akaroa Harbour. The Hamilton family has been custodian of this land since it was first sold to European immigrants in the nineteenth century. The area is of considerable significance because it was at Onuku, where a marae and village remain healthy to this day, that Maori chiefs on Banks Peninsula signed the Treaty of Waitangi, thus legalising the sale and purchase of land on the peninsula.

Jeff Hamilton has been farming people as well as a couple of thousand sheep for some years. He was astute enough to get into the backpacker business in its genesis, turning old farm buildings, including some that dated back to the 1850s, into a backpacker farm hostel that has young people from all over the world beating a path to its genuine kiwiana. Onuku Farm Hostel on Banks Peninsula, now run by Jeff's son Steve Hamilton, with added attractions such as sea-kayaking and dolphin swimming, is a must on any international backpacker's CV.

Banks Peninsula Track walkers stay in comfort in a purpose-built trampers' hut that would sleep the 12 walkers the trek is limited to. However, most don't bother to sleep there. Instead, they are likely to curl up inside funky small huts with glass roofs that expose the stars of the southern hemisphere. The stargazer huts are usually a deeply emotional experience for those who choose to sleep in them.

The 11 kilometre trek on day one starts as a bit of a toughie, involving a stiff climb to 699 metres, the highest point on the track. Fortunately, pack transport is available on the first day. At the summit there is a trig station point and, while you get your breath back, you can peer due west and on a clear day see the distinctive summit profile of Aoraki/Mt Cook poking up behind the front ranges of the Southern Alps, some 230 kilometres away.

From here it is downhill to Flea Bay through a remnant of the peninsula's native red beech forest that managed to escape fire and bush clearance because it is in a steep and narrow gully. The rest of Banks Peninsula was not so lucky, with just 600 hectares of the original 100,000 hectares of forest cover remaining. Immense land clearance fires that followed nineteenth-century logging are remembered as filling the entire Akaroa basin with smoke.

The bush, now protected by covenant, is part of the 650 hectares Helps' family property, a sheep and beef run farmed in partnership by brothers Francis and Steve Helps, and their wives Shireen and Pam. The farm was bought by their grandfather in 1916 but the family's peninsula credentials go back to 1858.

Flea Bay, farmed since 1843—the track accommodation

(Opposite) It is a bit of a grunt on the first day but the vista of Akaroa Harbour beneath your boots is always a good reason to take a break. Track accommodation ranges from backpacker chalets at Onuku (centre), to the quaint lodges built by Mark Armstrong at Stony Bay (top) and a nineteenth-century farm cottage at Flea Bay (bottom) that was the first home of Steve and Pam Helps.

is in one of the original farm cottages—is a deeply indented breach in the coastal ramparts with a safe shingle and sand beach from which bales of wool were ferried by lighter for shipment to Britain as early as 1846. It once supported three families, had its own school and a dairy where cheese and butter were made.

Now young Brits come to Flea Bay not to buy wool but to walk the route of the Banks Peninsula Track or witness the wildlife that passionate conservationists Francis and Shireen Helps are devoted to.

Flea Bay has always been a rich oasis: Maori mixed beach shingle with soil and built heat-attracting rock gardens so they could cultivate kumara 1000 kilometres further south than should really be possible. The bay is home to the largest New Zealand mainland colony of white-flippered penguins (a sub-species of the little blue), the rare yellow-eyed penguin, and fur seals. There are also Hector's dolphins close to shore. The waters around Flea Bay are protected in the Pohatu Marine Reserve, set up as a compromise between fishers, Ngai Tahu and conservationists, much to the Helps' delight. An optional extra for track walkers is to kayak around the bay, under Shireen's guidance, to see the wildlife close up. Elephant seals, sea lions and leopard seals are rare visitors

'We are farming conservation,' says Shireen Helps, who is midwife to over 1000 breeding pairs of penguins on a 91-hectare site just above the Helps' homestead. The nesting boxes, some at 200 metres above the sea, are mostly tiny wooden boxes, nestled into the hillside. 'The people who live on this coast are natural conservationists,' says Shireen. 'It is a beautiful place to live. The natural biodiversity is worth protecting.'

The second day of walking is a gentle 8 kilometre trail from Flea Bay to Stony Bay that follows the high-cliffed coastline to reveal one spectacular view after another. It is easy walking and the fit could knock it off in a couple of hours. But that would be a waste—you could easily spend that much time looking at the penguin nests above Flea

The track incorporates significant areas of native bush.

Bay and the young seal pups playing in Seal Cave. There are also sooty shearwater (muttonbirds) nesting sites on this section of the coast. When they were predated by stoats, a predator-proof fence was designed, financed and built by Mark Armstrong some ten years ago. It has been successful in helping to encourage more titi to breed.

The roads into Flea Bay and Stony Bay were only completed in the 1950s and are like the spokes of a wheel radiating from Akaroa. You may well have to carry your packs in this section—while you can always have your packs carted on the first and final days of the walk, and there is an option for groups to have them carted on days two and three, most carry theirs.

Mark Armstrong, whose newlywed parents arrived in Stony Bay on a horse-drawn sledge in 1940 to take over the farm that had been in the family since 1891, recalls being transported by packhorse, a child in a sack on each side of the horse. His father rode out to Akaroa every two weeks

BANKS PENINSULA TRACK, AKAROA, CANTERBURY

BANKS PENINSULA TRACK, AKAROA, CANTERBURY

for supplies and to pick up his children's correspondence school work.

Mark and his wife, Sonia, farm 3000 ewes on some 485 hectares, but the track and conservation work has become a big part of their lives and they have covenanted many hectares to the Queen Elizabeth II Trust as well as land to the Banks Peninsula Conservation Trust, formed by peninsula farmers. At Stony Bay you can't help but think Mark Armstrong is more artist than farmer. From the tree growing in the shower, to the toilet roll holder made from a cow horn and the open woodfire-heated bath, the accommodation here drips with character that a Hundertwasser or a Tolkien would surely appreciate.

It is hard to leave this oasis of whimsy and magic but day three's walk is another leisurely trek of 6 kilometres around the coast, past yellow-eyed penguins and frolicking fur seals to Otanerito (Long Bay), farmed by the Narbey family, who have been on the land since their ancestor François Narbey jumped ship in Akaroa in 1858. Accommodation for track walkers is in the beach house of Doug Hood and Fiona Farrell beside the sandy swimming beach.

The final day is a 10 kilometre trek through the Hinewai Reserve, climbing to a 600-metre saddle before descending to sea level again at Akaroa. The 1000-hectare native and regenerating bush reserve is private protected land, a permanent memorial to the altruistic spirit and conservation ethics of Banks Peninsula landowners.

(Pp. 166–167) A farm road makes its way around the coast at a pleasantly steady contour. Comfort is not forgotten either, with a privy conveniently sited in the wilderness.

(Top left) How better to soak away any aches and pains than in a hot tub heated by a wood fire? The individual chalet cooking facilities at Stony Bay (left) have the unmistakable touch of Mark Armstrong's handiwork.

The track passes through a little blue penguin rookery at Flea Bay and past a large fur seal nursery at Seal Cave (right).

Time Two or four-day options, both same distance
Length 35 kilometres
Type Farmland, bush, coastal
Start/finish Akaroa
Catering No
Pack carry On days one and four, as well as full pack cartage now available for groups
Special features Magnificent coastal scenery
Party number 12 on four-day; 4 on two-day
Accommodation Fully featured huts, lodge and farm cottage
Bedding Sleeping bags required
Season 1 October to 30 April
Further information www.bankstrack.co.nz; www.pohatu.co.nz; www.onukufarm.co.nz

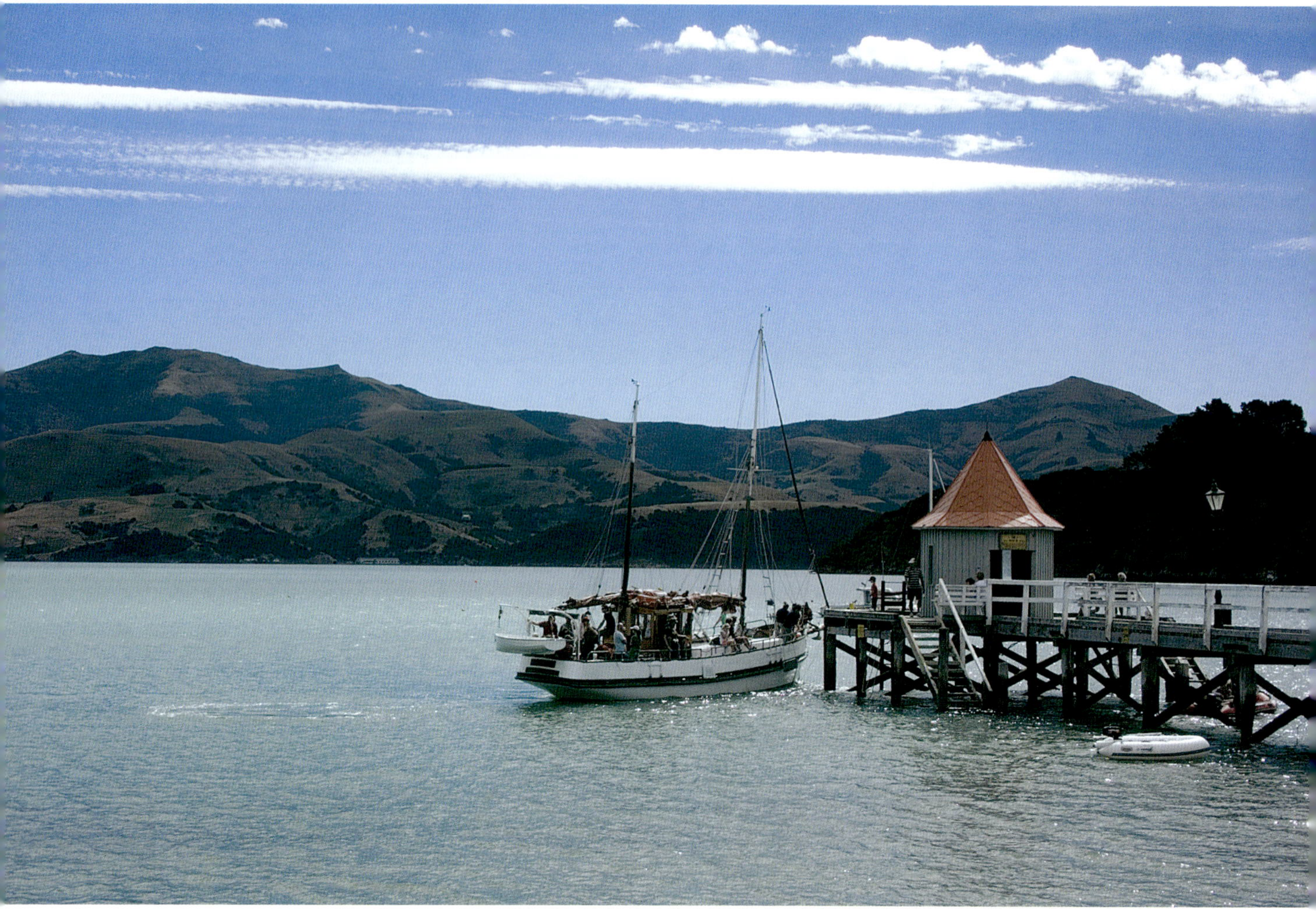

ISLAND TIME
THE AKAROA WALK, BANKS PENINSULA, CANTERBURY

Banks Peninsula sticks out of the east coast of the South Island like a closed fist. From 16 kilometres out at sea it can confuse even the most famous of navigators, luring Captain James Cook in 1770 to declare it Banks Island, after the celebrated botanist on his ship.

Some 20,000 years earlier it would have been an accurate description. Millions of years before, two enormous volcanoes, Lyttelton and Akaroa, had erupted out of the sea, reaching up to 2000 metres in height and spewing lava in a huge radius like the volcanic islands of Hawaii.

The eruptions stopped about six million years ago and the volcanoes might have remained an island had not debris from the eroding tops of the Southern Alps been carried to the coast by Ice Age glaciers and rivers to give the island a wrist and create a peninsula.

While the land link to the mainland may put Banks Peninsula in easy reach of Christchurch, it remains a volcanic island in all but name. So a traverse from one enormous eruption basin, now a harbour, to the other is actually a walk across Banks 'island'.

The Akaroa Walk, which crosses the 100,000 hectare peninsula roughly from north to south, differs from other private walks in that it is the creation of an adventure travel company. Tuatara Tours has considerable experience in running guided walks on several noted South Island tracks but, unlike those other tracks, the Akaroa Walk is a distinct creation.

It is a fully guided walk, which is probably just as well because, more than any other of the private walks, the Akaroa adventure is a trek through a fascinating montage of history. The guides, mostly experienced and semi-retired trampers, bring to life the cameos from the past that the track traverses.

It is also probably the closest New Zealand walk to the inn-to-inn walks of Europe, with excellent accommodation and food provided every night. You have to walk for your supper but you will be pampered when you get there.

The 42 kilometre trek across the peninsula's hilltops begins in Christchurch with a gondola ride to the summit ridge of the city's Port Hills, the northern rim of the Lyttelton volcanic crater that gives the otherwise featureless metropolis some physical definition.

After the first latte of the day, it is off on an easy 9 kilometre walk on the Crater Rim Walkway, high above Lyttelton Harbour, and on to Godley Head on the Godley Head Walkway. There are Second World War gun emplacements on the heads that fortunately never fired a shot in anger.

Akaroa Harbour is one of the most picturesque in the country with tour boats and a wharf in keeping with its flavour.

For the route along the summit ridge of the Port Hills you can thank the vision of Harry Ell, who in the first few decades of the twentieth century campaigned tirelessly for a continuous path linking a series of bush reserves from Godley Head to Gebbies Pass and around the peninsula hills to Akaroa. Ell opened a series of roadhouses along the route.

A shuttle pickup makes a short detour to Lyttelton's historic Timeball Station, built in 1876 to signal Greenwich Mean Time to shipping in the harbour, and one of only five in the world still working. Walkers then catch a commuter ferry to Diamond Harbour and accommodation for the first night, Godley House.

The stately home, built in 1880, has been magnificently

restored as a boutique hotel and restaurant—just the place to relax in comfort after a day out walking.

You need the rest because day two is a 22 kilometre trek over the heights of Banks Peninsula, traversing around Mt Fitzgerald at 826 metres and Mt Sinclair at 844 metres.

It is an undulating ridge-top walk that, while not too arduous, fills out much of the day. But the toil is rewarded with views that would shame an Imax cinema. It is here that the Akaroa Walk guide comes in mighty handy—as does the comprehensive booklet on the history of Banks Peninsula given to each walker. Every bay and indent that lies around the coast like the teeth on a giant cog has a fascinating story of Maori occupation and pioneering European farming.

As the day wears on, the trail, mostly over old farm tracks once used as pack tracks between Diamond Harbour and Akaroa, reveals constantly changing aspects until at Hilltop, Akaroa Harbour comes into full and dramatic view.

Trekkers arrive at the Akaroa Walk's Pentrip Lodge, and to a much-deserved cold beverage and a hot spa for you to soak and relax your hard-worked body.

Set on 7.8 hectares of grounds, Pentrip Lodge has well-appointed rooms and beautiful gardens. It is a new home on the site of one of the peninsula's nineteenth-century stately homesteads. The last family member was something of an eccentric who would walk to the local pub in dressing gown and slippers. When he died his male partner stayed on the 200 hectare farm, taking up with a woman and a clutch of children. When he died the rest of the family finally reclaimed the property but not before a mysterious fire in 1997 gutted the 1880s homestead. Pentrip Lodge was built from the insurance, subdivided and the farm sold.

Dinner will likely include Akaroa smoked salmon, with local wine and produce, served on the deck or by the fire.

Day three begins near Hilltop at the Montgomery native

Once huge volcanic craters, Lyttelton Harbour (top right and centre) and Akaroa Harbour (left) are both crossed on the Akaroa Walk. Godley House (bottom right and overleaf top) was built in 1880 and has now been restored as a boutique hotel and restaurant.

The delightfully quaint township of Akaroa shows its French heritage with pavement cafés and fine dining.

THE AKAROA WALK, BANKS PENINSULA, CANTERBURY 175

176 THE AKAROA WALK, BANKS PENINSULA, CANTERBURY

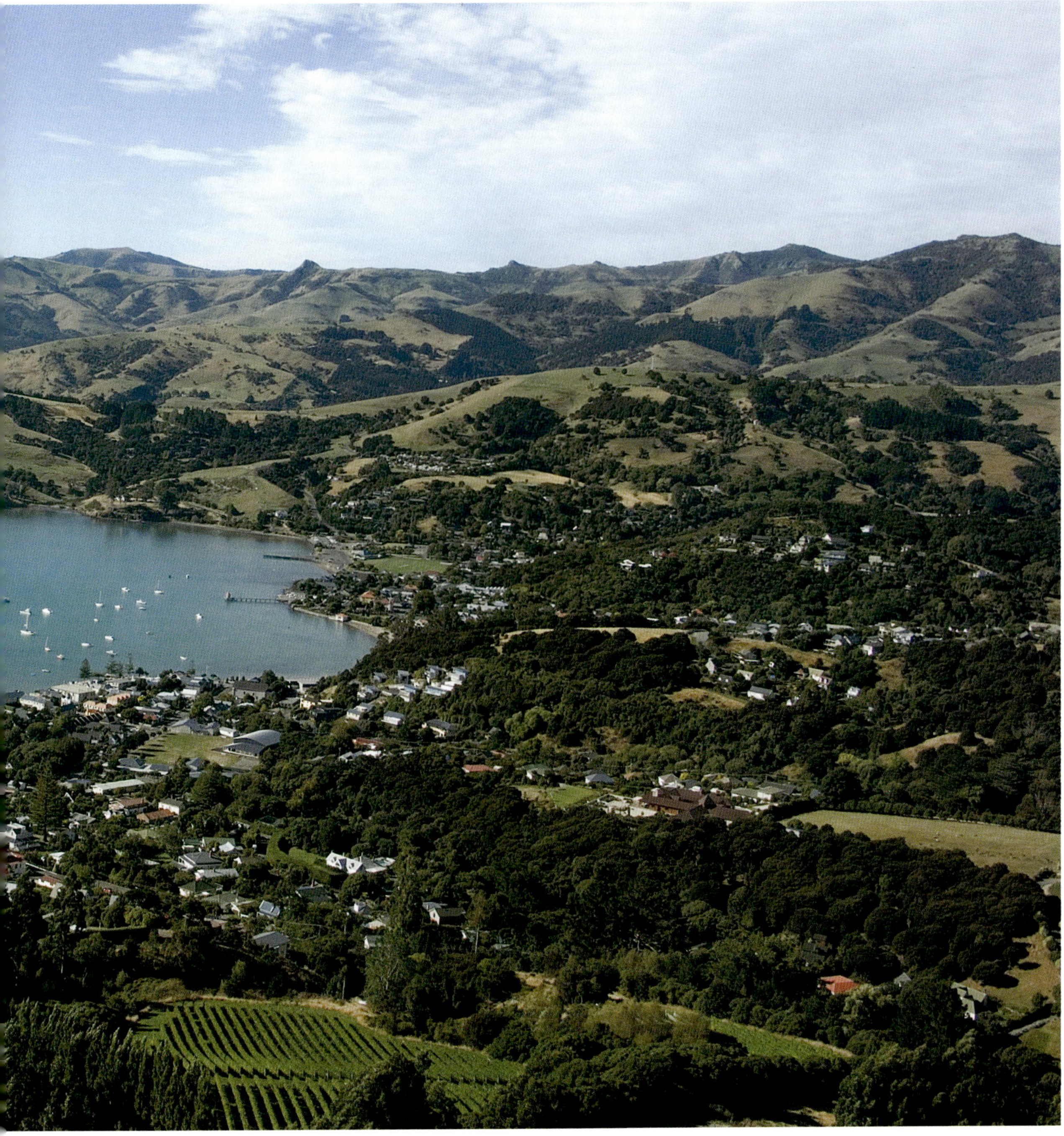

bush reserve, which contains a 2000-year-old totara that is thought to be the oldest living tree on Banks Peninsula.

Akaroa Harbour lies deceptively in view but there are 11 kilometres of walking to do first, beginning, if you wish, with a short climb to the top of French Hill, 815 metres above the harbour. You can opt to simply traverse it.

From there it is a gentle descent through lush farming valleys to Wainui, where a ferry takes you across the harbour to at last rub shoulders with the charms of Akaroa. You have the rest of the afternoon to discover the delightful French settlement at your own leisure. Wander the streets and explore the boutique shops, local art and cafés. There is also a wide range of accommodation to choose from.

Later in the evening the group gathers at a fine-dining waterfront café for a celebration dinner with your guide.

The following morning you can enjoy breakfast at one of the many cafés and look out at French Hill in the knowledge that the previous day you were at the top looking down on Akaroa. A shuttle brings you back to Christchurch, arriving at midday, or you can extend your time in Akaroa and catch a later shuttle back.

The Crater Rim Walkway (top left) to Godley Head begins the Akaroa Walk. From Hilltop, Akaroa Harbour is deceptively in view but there is an 11 kilometre trek to get there—a good reason for a rest above the clouds (above) along the way. Wild flowers brighten the roadside above Taylors Mistake (left). (Pp. 176–177) Akaroa is a living memorial to French settlers with its streets named in French and many of its buildings retaining a French flavour.

Time Three days, three nights
Length 42 kilometres
Type Pasture, coastal, native bush
Start/finish Christchurch
Catering Yes
Pack carry Yes
Special features Fully guided, fine dining
Party number 12
Accommodation Fully serviced lodges
Bedding Provided
Season 1 November 1 to 30 April
Further information www.tuataratours.co.nz

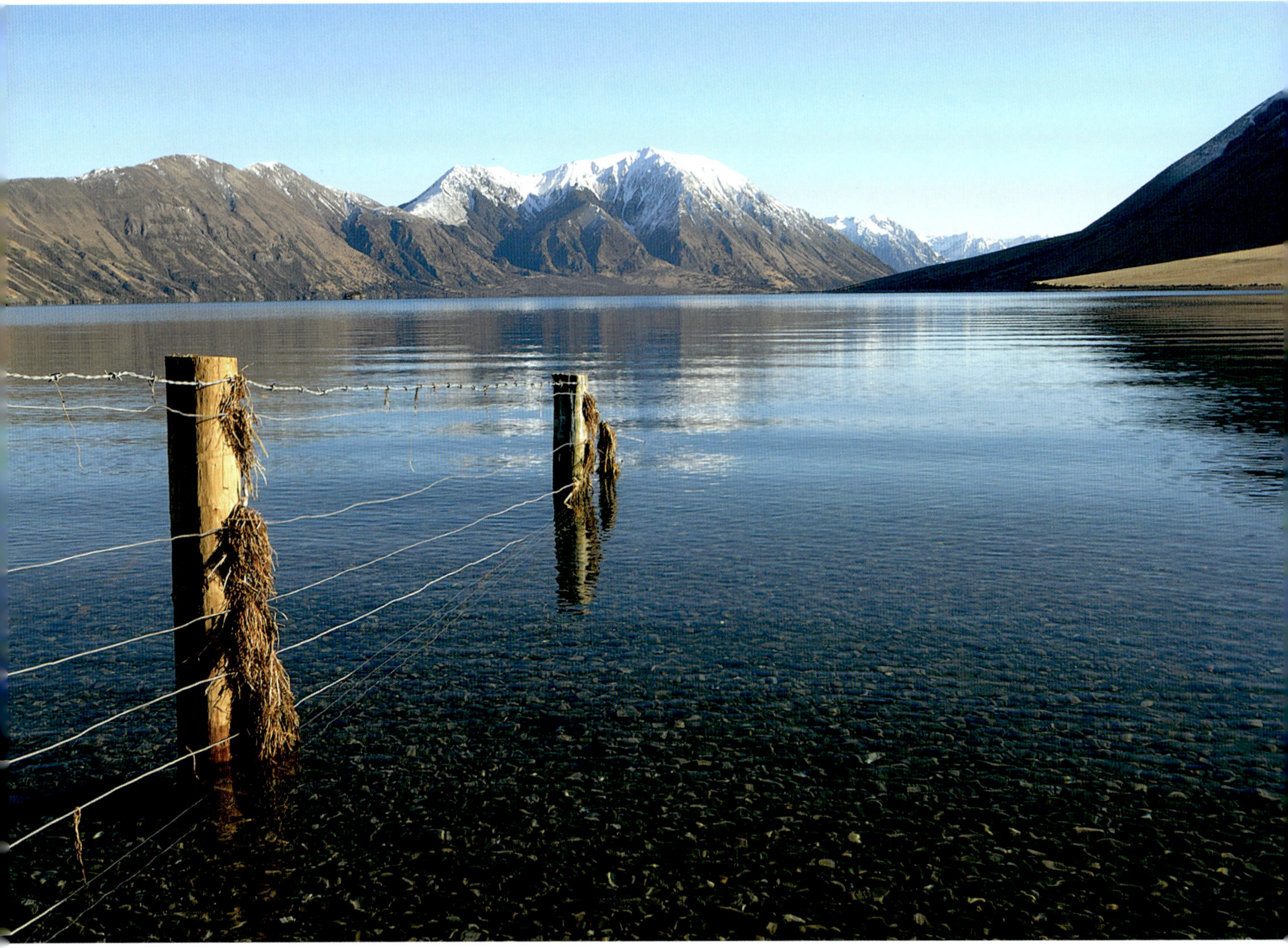

WALKING IN SPACE
GLENTHORNE STATION HIGH COUNTRY WALKS, LAKE COLERIDGE

The sense of space in the Lake Coleridge basin is overwhelming. The land seems to go on forever, and in every direction there are soaring mountains and rolling, tussock-clad hills, their faces etched by barren scree slopes, their colour forever changing with the passage of the sun and shade.

The land rolls on until in the distance it reaches the snow-capped peaks of the Southern Alps on the Main Divide. It is a land that swallows you into insignificance in the river flats carved between the hills by ancient glaciers. This is the New Zealand outback, a land that inspired Samuel Butler's nineteenth-century novel *Erewhon* and was immortalised by pioneering settler Mona Anderson in *A river rules my life*.

At its centre lies Glenthorne Station, a 26,000 hectare high-country station, bounded by the north-east shores of Lake Coleridge, the Wilberforce River and the Craigieburn Range, whose eastern flanks are home to a clutch of ski areas. Just to the west, feeding into the Harper and then the Rakaia Rivers, are the legendary Wilberforce and Avoca Rivers, rugged pathways into the Alps used by generations of hardy trampers.

Follow the Harper River and you will reach the Cass-Lagoon Saddle circuit in Craigieburn Forest Park, one of the most popular weekend tramps in the South Island. To the east is the 22,000 hectare Korowai/Torlesse Tussocklands Park, New Zealand's first tussock grasslands park, established as a result of the tenure review process and opened in November 2001.

Glenthorne Station lies about as close to the centre of the South Island as you can get—the west coast is 100 kilometres away, the east 110 kilometres. Fortunately, the wide open spaces of Glenthorne have not been locked away just for the benefit of the property's 13,000 Merino sheep and 450 cattle. The dramatic landscape and spectacularly clear days are shared with a range of tourism opportunities, from four-wheel-drive trails to soaking up the grandeur of the place, with accommodation ranging from the comfort of modern ensuite chalets with all meals provided to a choice of five fully furnished self-catering facilities.

From these various places guests can fish from five lakes and two major rivers nearby, play golf on the international Terrace Downs course just 20 minutes away, go horse trekking, or begin the Station-to-Station, five-day,

Lakes, rivers and mountains and 26,000 hectares of fine tramping country are housed in Glenthorne Station.

A stunning view of Mt Ida in the foreground with the snow-clad peaks of Blue Hill, home of Porter Heights skifield, in the background

six-night-self-drive-four-wheel drive tour through several adjoining high-country stations. The Mt Olympus skifield of the Windwhistle Winter Sports Club is within Glenthorne's boundaries, and the Mt Hutt, Porter Heights, Mt Cheeseman, Craigieburn and Broken River skifields are close by. Glenthorne Station Walks is a series of marked walking trails, ranging in length from an hour or two to all-day tramps. Each trail has its own distinctive features and different points of geological or botanical interest. They also vary from easy to demanding, with some climbing from the accommodation, which is at 550 metres, to 1000 metres.

Round Hill, not far from Lower Glenthorne station buildings, is perfectly named. Its contour lines rise in symmetrical steps until they reach the summit at 898 metres. Between Round Hill and the oblong and slightly higher Laings Hill is a tussock valley and scrub of spindly kanuka, coprosma and matagouri. Both the valley track circumnavigating Round Hill or a climb up and over the summit take about two and a half hours. From the summit, there are extensive views over Glenthorne Station and Lake Coleridge, so be sure to take the time to sign your name in the summit book. To the north-east, Blue Hill dominates the skyline. Hidden in a basin behind the twin summits that reach to nearly 2000 metres is the Porter Heights skifield.

Mt Hennah, another stand-alone peak, across the Ryton River to the north of Round Hill, is 1109 metres high, and its three-hour marked walk focuses on walking around the base, with a visit to a stunning waterfall. A walk to the neighbouring peak, Carriage Drive (1055 metres), focuses on a sheep-mustering trail.

The Goldney Circuit is an all-day wilderness tramp from the Lower Glenthorne homestead to Goldney Hill at the foot of Blue Hill. This is a spectacularly rugged and barren landscape, much ravaged by the violent collision of tectonic plates and erosion. Blue Hill is now perhaps just one-third of its former height, its slopes littered with millions of cubic metres of rock from what is believed to have been an enormous rock avalanche.

Two other all-day walks are probably best done using a vehicle shuttle. The Clay Range is the moraine wall at the junction of two glacial valleys that follow the fault lines and are now the route of the Harper and Avoca Rivers. A 17 kilometre trail circumnavigating this range of clay drops down into the Harper near the confluence of the Avoca. On the north bank the glacial clay has been eroded into 'badlands' pinnacles. The energetic can cross the river for a closer look. The Clay Range circuit includes the delightful Mystery Tarn, a small alpine lake, and, on the return, a small lake the locals call Lake Monck but which is shown on topo maps as Lake Catherine. There is an old musterers' hut here that is perfectly habitable and is a fine place for a brew-up out of the wind.

You could also spend a long day walking around the Cottons Sheep Range, returning along the slopes that run down into Lake Coleridge. However, it probably makes more sense to cut the trip to about four hours and get driven to the end of Harper Road, which leads down to

The area is home to Mt Olympus, a club ski area, and Lake Ida, which usually freezes over in winter and in the past was used for curling events. Lower Glenthorne has private en suite chalets (top), or at the other extreme there is Monck Hut, an old musterers' cabin (centre) which makes for a good spot to stop at the end of the all-day Clay Range walk.

GLENTHORNE STATION HIGH COUNTRY WALKS, LAKE COLERIDGE

the canals that feed Lake Coleridge with water from the Harper and Wilberforce Rivers. A track leads up to a lookout with extensive views over fields by the canals and back into the vast reaches of the upper Wilberforce. The trail back to the Lower Glenthorne accommodation follows an easy contour above the stunning blue waters of Lake Coleridge, until eventually dropping down to the shoreline near the Ryton River. The wetland flats where the Ryton River flows into the lake are thick with waterfowl, some of them birds that migrate between nesting areas in braided South Island rivers and the coastal beaches and estuaries of the North Island.

Even the birds seem to emphasise the variety and eclectic nature of the walks available at Glenthorne Station,

The Harper River winds its way past Mt Ida at the beginning of the Lakeside walk to the lookout.

whether it's an easy half hour botanical introduction on the Eco walk, or a gentle lakeside stroll from the homestead to the peninsula and back.

No matter what accommodation you're in at Glenthorne Station, they all have stunning mountaing views, while some look down on the royal blue waters of Lake Coleridge. The lake was formed by glacier moraine which left a height difference of 170 metres between Lake Coleridge and the Rakaia River. This meant it was an ideal site for the country's first state hydroelectric scheme, using some diverted water from the Harper and Wilberforce Rivers. The power station

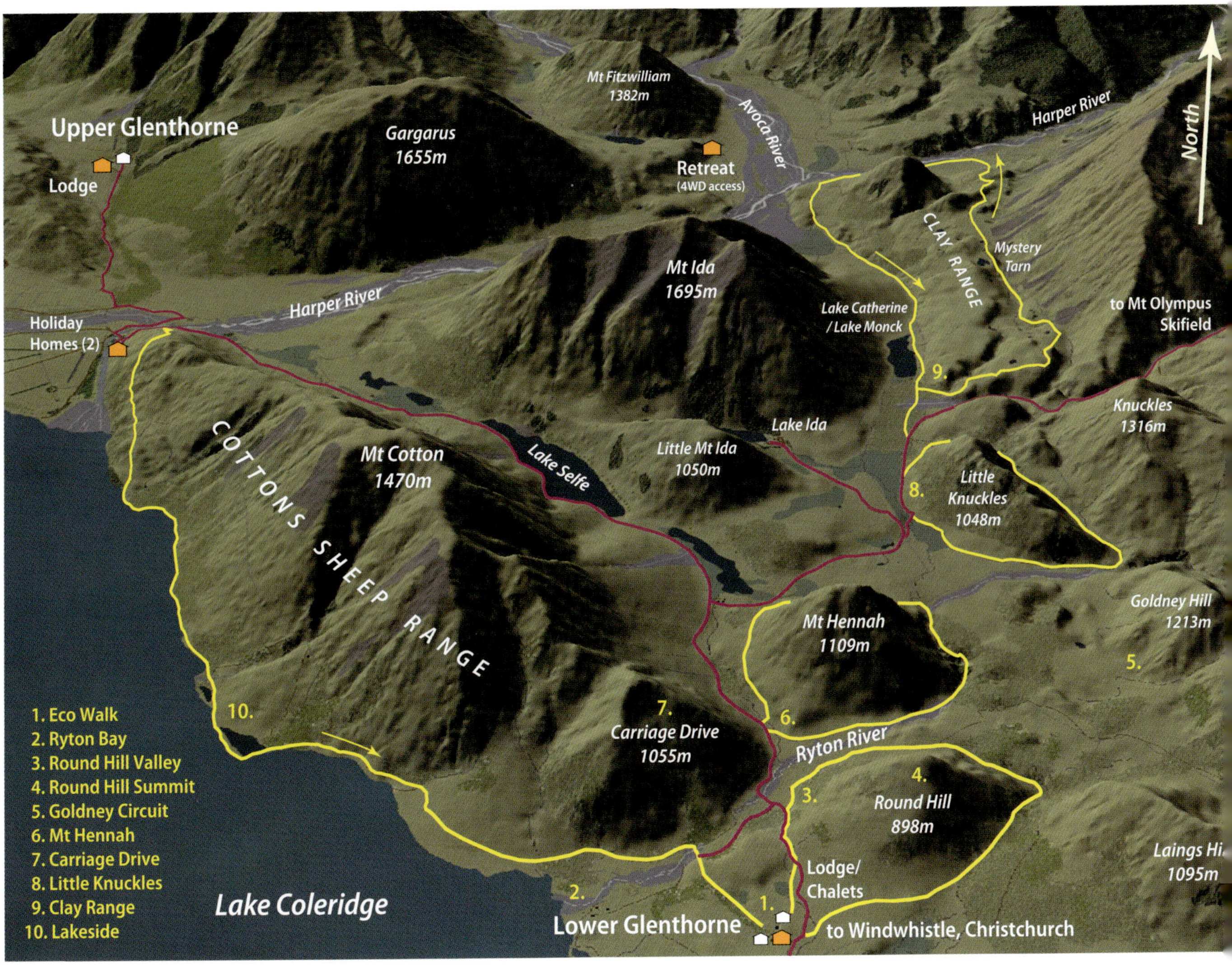

Upper Glenthorne
Lodge
Gargarus
1655m
Mt Fitzwilliam
1382m
Avoca River
Retreat
(4WD access)
Harper River
North
Mt Ida
1695m
CLAY RANGE
Mystery
Tarn
Lake Catherine
/ Lake Monck
to Mt Olympus
Skifield
Harper River
Holiday
Homes (2)
9.
Knuckles
1316m
COTTONS SHEEP RANGE
Mt Cotton
1470m
Lake Selfe
Little Mt Ida
1050m
Lake Ida
8.
Little
Knuckles
1048m
Goldney Hill
1213m
Mt Hennah
1109m
5.
10.
7.
Carriage Drive
1055m
6.
Ryton River
4.
3.
Round Hill
898m
Laings Hi
1095m
Lodge/
Chalets
2.
1.
Lake Coleridge
Lower Glenthorne
to Windwhistle, Christchurch
1. Eco Walk
2. Ryton Bay
3. Round Hill Valley
4. Round Hill Summit
5. Goldney Circuit
6. Mt Hennah
7. Carriage Drive
8. Little Knuckles
9. Clay Range
10. Lakeside

GLENTHORNE STATION HIGH COUNTRY WALKS, LAKE COLERIDGE

GLENTHORNE STATION HIGH COUNTRY WALKS, LAKE COLERIDGE

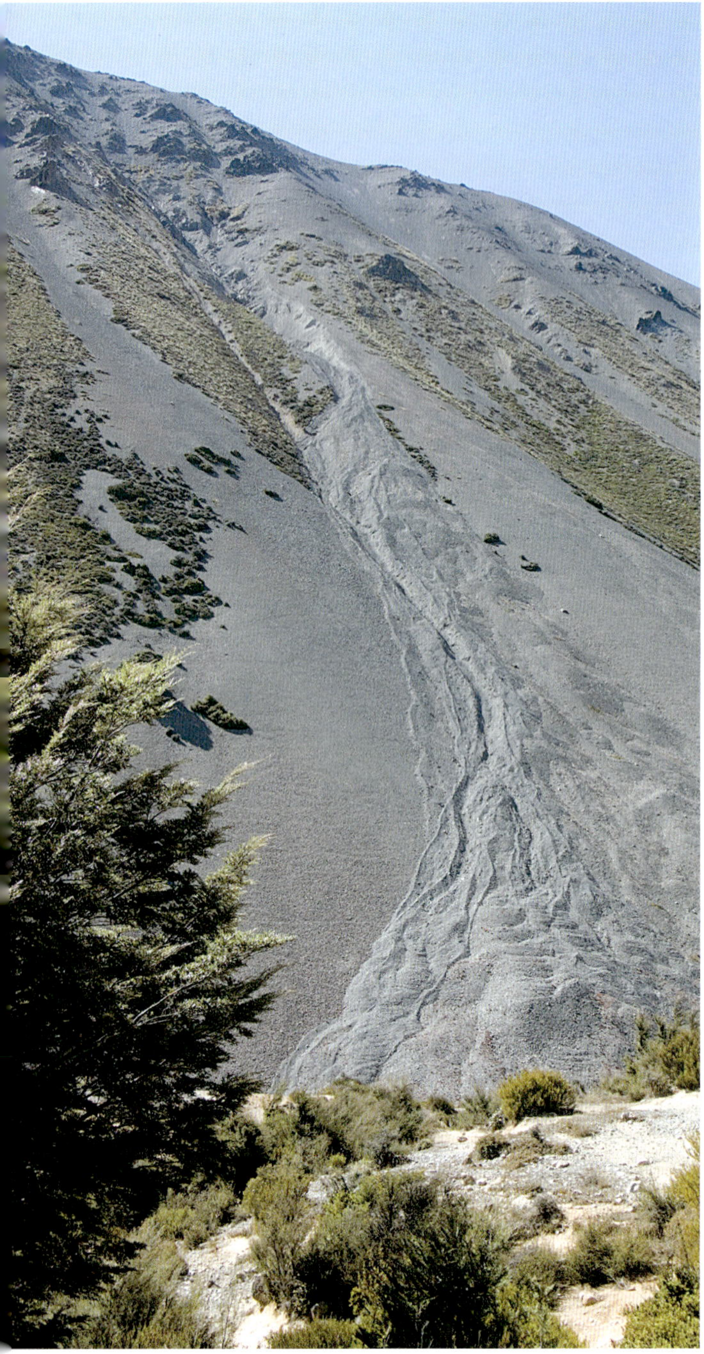

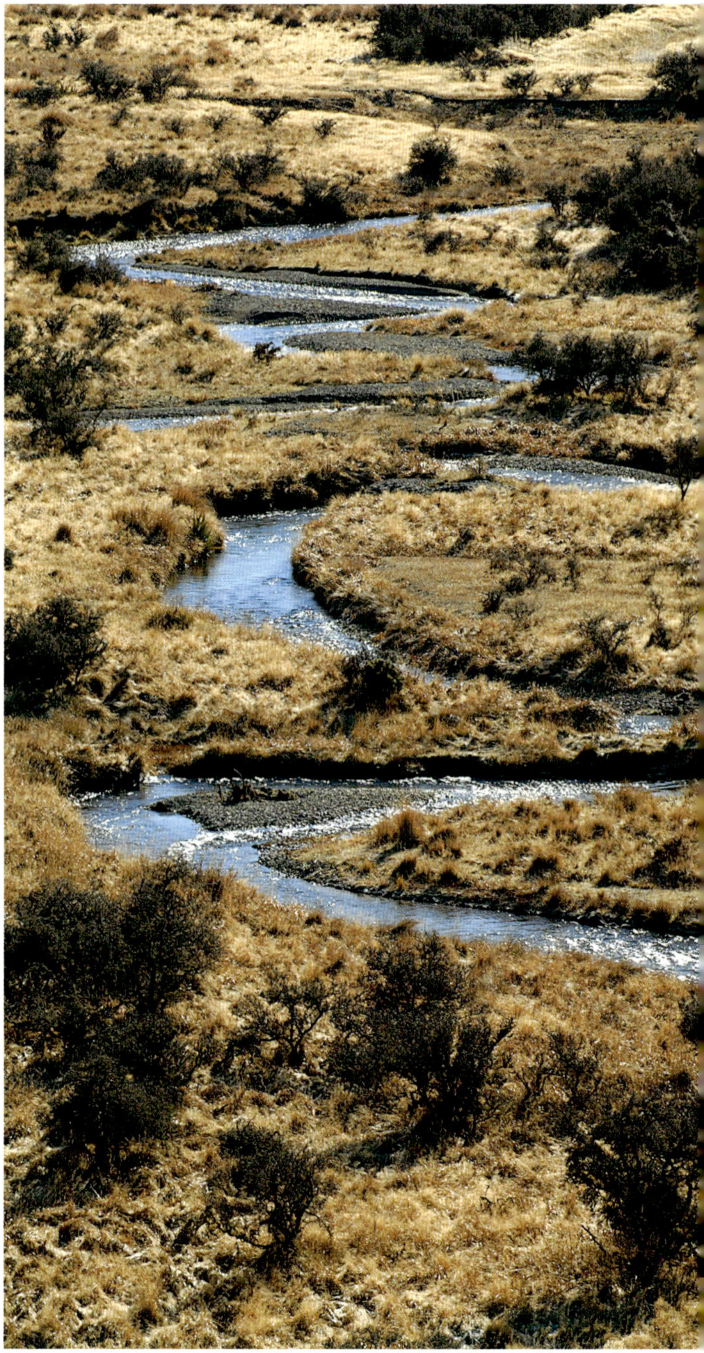

Time Three to four days
Length Range of walks from one hour to all day
Type Mostly high country tussock, herbfields
Start/finish Most walks based at the Lower Glenthorne side of the station
Catering Yes, in chalets only
Pack carry Not required
Special features Clear air, soaring hills, magnificent views
Party number Up to 30, depending on accommodation choice
Accommodation Chalets, lodge, holidays houses, retreat
Bedding Provided in chalets; self-catering on request
Season Year round
Further information www.glenthorne.co.nz

was completed in 1914 and, although small by modern standards, still feeds power into the national grid.

Nowadays the lake and its surrounding basin are better known as a tourism centre for outdoor activities. A steady north-west wind makes Lake Coleridge a favoured wind surfing venue. The lake area is also renowned for good salmon and trout fishing, with either fly or spinner.

Be careful out there, however. In her book *New Zealand Mysteries*, Robyn Gosset mentions a rash of sightings during the 1970's of 'Lakey', a large animal living in the lake. No reports have emerged since!

Glenthorne is a landscape photographer or artist's nirvana with stunning vistas in every direction, vibrant colours and endless contrasts from scree slopes (far left), golden tussock and trout streams, and snow-capped peaks. (Pp. 186–187) Mystery Lake, an alpine tarn with no visible inlet or outlet.

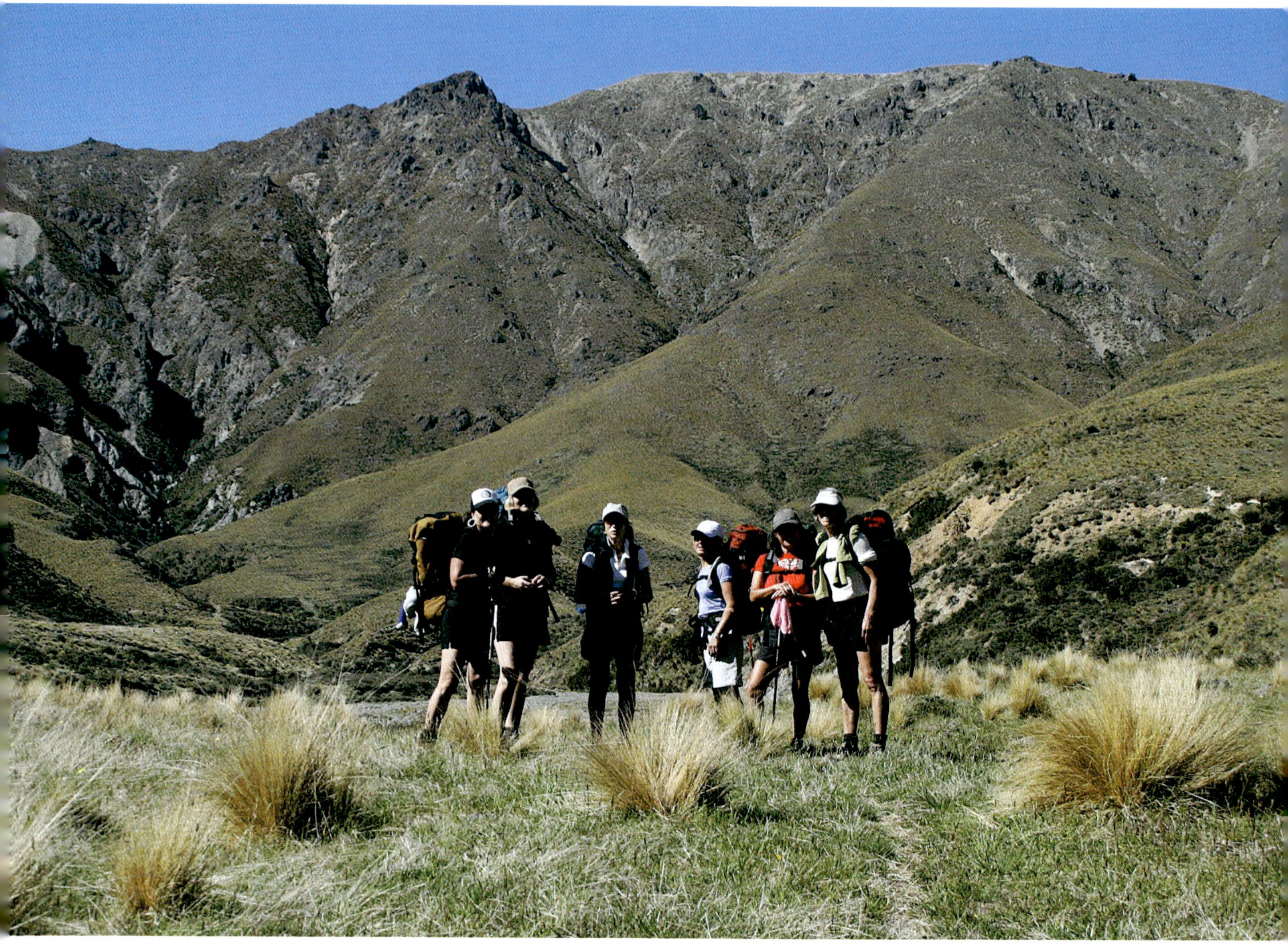

HEART OF THE HIGH COUNTRY
FOUR PEAKS HIGH COUNTRY TRACK, GERALDINE, SOUTH CANTERBURY

*The essentials of station life in New Zealand have probably changed little from the days in the 1860s when Lady Barker wrote her classic account of the life of farmers in the South Island high country—*Station Life in New Zealand. *Rivers still flood, sheep get lost in snowstorms, and drought is a constant threat.*

Loneliness still has to be contended with, prices for stock are more down than up, while those for essential supplies are more up than down. Yet, according to the anecdotal stereotype, anyone farming more than 4000 hectares and some 8000 ewes on traditional high country such as Lady Barker lived on commutes to town by helicopter, sends their children to exclusive boarding schools and likely plays polo. Some do, of course, but the reality is much closer to the sheer hard work that Lady Barker described. And nowhere is that more evident than at Oregon, the 324 hectare farm of Jo and Steve McAtamney, on the mid-Canterbury plains at Carew, and on their 4050 hectare high-country station, Four Peaks, inland from Geraldine, in South Canterbury.

If you had to find dinkum red and black Cantabrians, you couldn't go past the McAtamney family. Their comfortable, yet homely, abode reeks of the Crusaders and Canterbury rugby, inspired no doubt by sons, Daniel, Matt

Tussock hills and high peaks laced with scree slopes— country that defines South Island tramping

and Josh, but encouraged by mum and dad, too. These are community people, who support the local schools and sports clubs, but who are also farmers. Both Steve and Jo are from Canterbury farming families, facing the age-old problems of people on the land—hard work and not a lot of money to show for it.

Oregon, with its sheep, beef and deer, has given the McAtamneys a good life but it is subject to drought. So in 2001 the couple realised a dream and bought Four Peaks Station to give their farming operation the flexibility of high-country tussock and plains pasture, working in tandem as breeding and fattening units. With the station came three old musterers' huts, much run-down and badly in need of some TLC, but reeking of character and the history of 150 years of use. Originally the McAtamneys wanted to do them up and make them more comfortable for their initial purpose—mustering. 'We enjoy mustering and staying in these remote spots as a family,' says Jo McAtamney. But how could they justify the expense, particularly after a disastrous winter in 2006 left the farm budget in tatters?

Then the couple, keen outdoors folks and regular trampers themselves, remembered the good time they had had a few years before, walking the Banks Peninsula Track.

Thus was born the Four Peaks High Country Track, a 40 kilometre circuit over genuine high-country tussock, with passes and peaks, ups and downs, big country views, solitude … and those three shepherds' huts. If Steve McAtamney ever decides to give up farming he should find ready work in the restoration of old buildings. The run-down hovels he inherited are now beautifully restored and offer comfortable accommodation, without having sacrificed any of the huts' original character.

Cloud sits on the topmost ridge at Four Peaks. It may be raining on one side of the ridge and fine and clear on the other.

The first one you'll stay in is Pleasant Gully Hut, just 20 minutes' walk from the road end, upstream from Te Moana Gorge, where walkers are dropped in the late afternoon after a briefing from Jo McAtamney. Built in the late 1890s—the earliest autograph found etched in the original timber was in 1902—the hut looks much like the ageing corrugated-iron shelter the McAtamneys inherited, but its looks are a little deceiving. After more than a century of use, Pleasant

Gully Hut was in a sad condition, with borer-infested and rotten timber. Steve totally rebuilt its internal framing and basic structure, then replaced the old clay used for insulation with modern glass-fibre insulation, lined the walls with Oregon and macrocarpa, re-piled the foundations, gave the scrim bunks spring bases with mattresses, and repaired the open fireplace and stone chimney. It is built of dressed river stones and is two metres wide at the base, tapering to its three-metre height.

A good fire has always been essential at Pleasant Gully for cooking, drying wet clothes and keeping shepherds warm from the chills found at 450 metres. It was considered the most important of all the Four Peaks Station huts, serving as a base hut and used three times more often than the other musterers' huts. The four or five-day muster would usually begin and end with a night at Pleasant Gully. Among the graffiti scratched on the hut timbers was the name of a distant relative. 'It makes us feel like we are doing the right thing,' says Jo McAtamney.

Having spent the night absorbing the high-country station atmosphere, it is time for some serious walking, 15 kilometres, mostly over natural stock tracks used during mustering, that will take five to six hours. The climb to Fiery Pass at 1284 metres is long and steady, through bush, river bed and tussock. If you want to check your fitness against that of the old-time shepherds, you can do so at the Hour Mark at 823 metres. It is a good place to stop for a breather and contemplate that musterers were supposed to get here in no more than an hour from Pleasant Gully Hut. If they didn't, it was considered that they wouldn't be up to handling the next six days of the muster and were sent back to the hut to pack up supplies.

Before the last climb to the pass you can fill your water bottles with crystal-clear water from a tributary of the Hae Hae Te Moana River. No domestic stock are grazed upstream.

Huts that have given shelter to shepherds from storms for decades have been imaginatively restored to their homely and rustic best to become cosy tramping accommodation.

FOUR PEAKS HIGH COUNTRY TRACK, GERALDINE, SOUTH CANTERBURY

FOUR PEAKS HIGH COUNTRY TRACK, GERALDINE, SOUTH CANTERBURY

Further on, another block has been retired from grazing and between February and March clumps of alpine gentians and mountain rock daisies flower alongside the track. Fiery Pass is worth spending a little time at and not just because it has been a bit of a slog to get there. The view is startling—to the east you can see as far as the Port Hills above Christchurch, while in the foreground the Geraldine Forest covers the Waitohi Range. Then follow the compass south through Geraldine, Temuka, Timaru, Pleasant Point, to the Hunter Hills of Waimate, with the Fonterra milk plant at Clandeboye on the Canterbury Plains towards the Pacific Ocean coast.

Turn to the west and Fox Peak stands tall at 2300 metres on the left of the Clayton Range, with the Two Thumb Range around to the right.

But, as photogenic as the view may be, of particular interest are the quite noticeable differences in landscape and climate on either side of Fiery Pass. Often it can be raining on the east side yet fine and sunny on the west looking to the Mackenzie Country. The farm stock also do better on the warmer and drier country where the grass must grow sweeter.

A steep downhill on a farm road brings you to Sutherland's Hut, built on the banks of the Mowbray River in 1866 by a Devonshire stonemason, James Radford. It was one of 14 huts, five of which were built in stone, that were spread around the Orari Gorge Station's 27,450 hectares.

Huts like Sutherland's were used by shepherds for mustering and boundary keeping in the days when little of the high country was fenced. They were used consistently up until the 1970s, when four-wheel drive tracks were pushed into the backcountry.

Sutherland was a shepherd on the Orari Gorge Station with the lonely job of spending several weeks after the main

From Jumpover Saddle (pp. 194–195) there are extensive views across the Fairlie Basin to the snow-covered peaks of the Southern Alps.

(Left) On a clear day you can look across the Canterbury Plains to the Pacific Ocean coast.

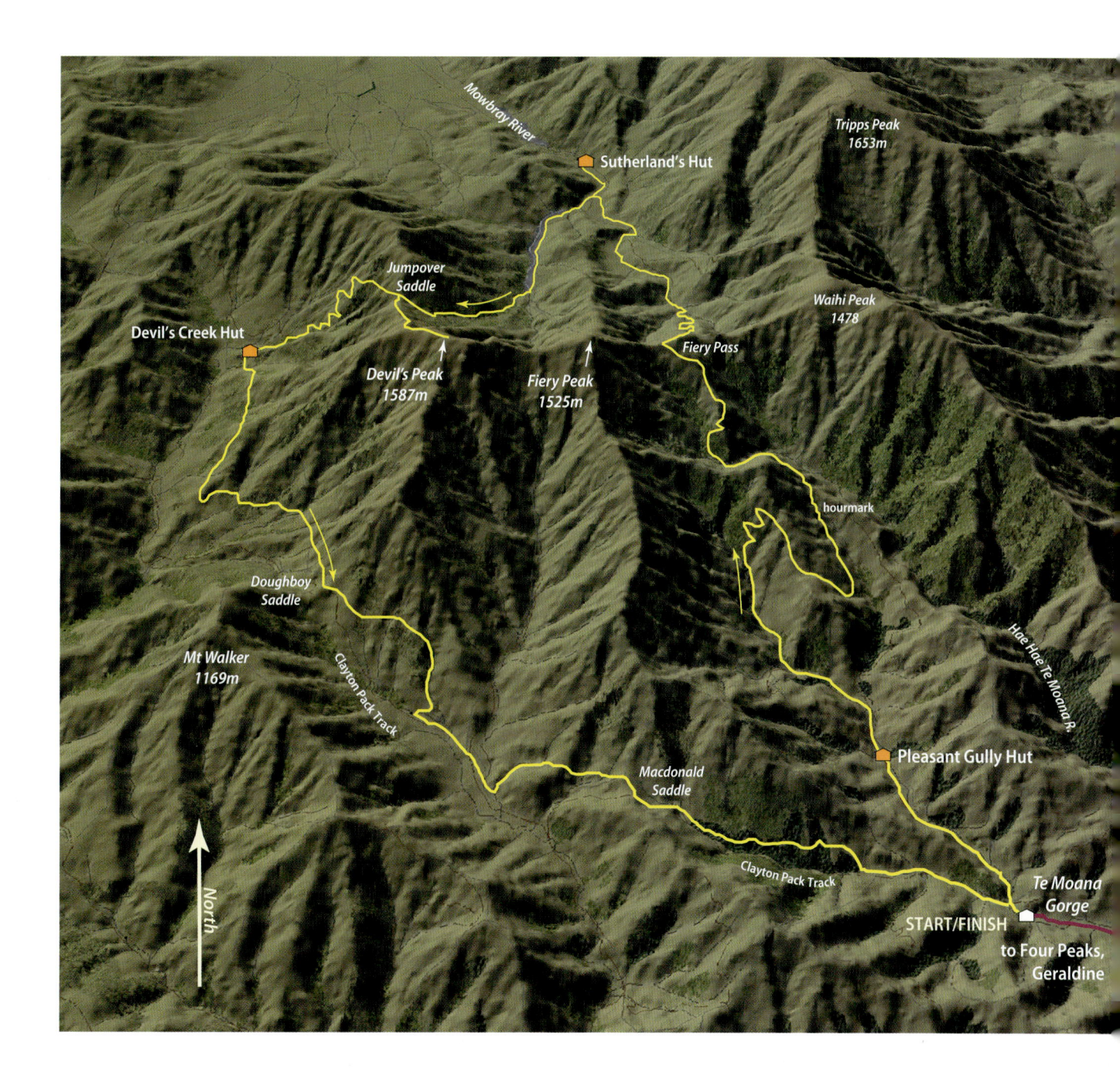

FOUR PEAKS HIGH COUNTRY TRACK, GERALDINE, SOUTH CANTERBURY

muster rounding up any stragglers, with only his horse and dogs for company. The original hut was built with stones from the Mowbray River, with a tussock-thatched roof and a dirt floor. The stone walls have been substantially repaired and the interior lined with Oregon timber. Like all the huts on the Four Peaks walk, this heritage hut is conveniently sited near running water just deep enough in places to lie in.

Day two of nine kilometres begins with a gentle stroll up the river bed before the going gets tough up the aptly named climbs—The Snort, The Buster and The Grunt. Ahead lies Jumpover Saddle at 1151 metres and views beyond Lake Opuha into the Fairlie Basin, Mackenzie Country, and to the skifields of Fox Peak and Mt Dobson. Those who have managed to snort their way up The Grunt without getting busted can get an even better view from the top of Devil's Peak at 1587 metres, a detour that will add about two and a half hours to the day.

It may be uphill (right), but without a pack to carry it is not too much of a slog. Alpine wild flowers bloom in spring and stock are kept away from some areas so that the colourful display can survive. Accommodation is provided at Pleasant Gully Hut (top left) and Sutherland's Hut (bottom left).

Home for the night is Devil's Creek Hut, sited in peaceful isolation and still frequently used for mustering. It was originally built in 1870 but was burnt down and replaced in the 1930s.

Day three is a 15 kilometre long walk sidling around the foot of Devil's Peak not far above the Clayton Pack Track, formed in the 1800s to give access to the Fairlie Basin from Geraldine and still clearly visible. The highest point of the day is Doughboy Saddle at 842 metres. The last couple of kilometres to the road end where the walk began three days earlier is on the Clayton Pack Track—which seems a thoroughly appropriate way to end a walk on a high-country station where stock have grazed for more than 150 years.

Time Three days, three nights
Length 40 kilometres
Type High-country tussockland
Start/finish Four Peaks Station, Geraldine
Catering No
Pack carry Yes
Special features Genuine high country farming
Party number Eight
Accommodation Restored musterers' huts, fully equipped
Bedding Yes (just bring sleeping bag)
Season November to April
Further information www.walkfourpeaks.co.nz

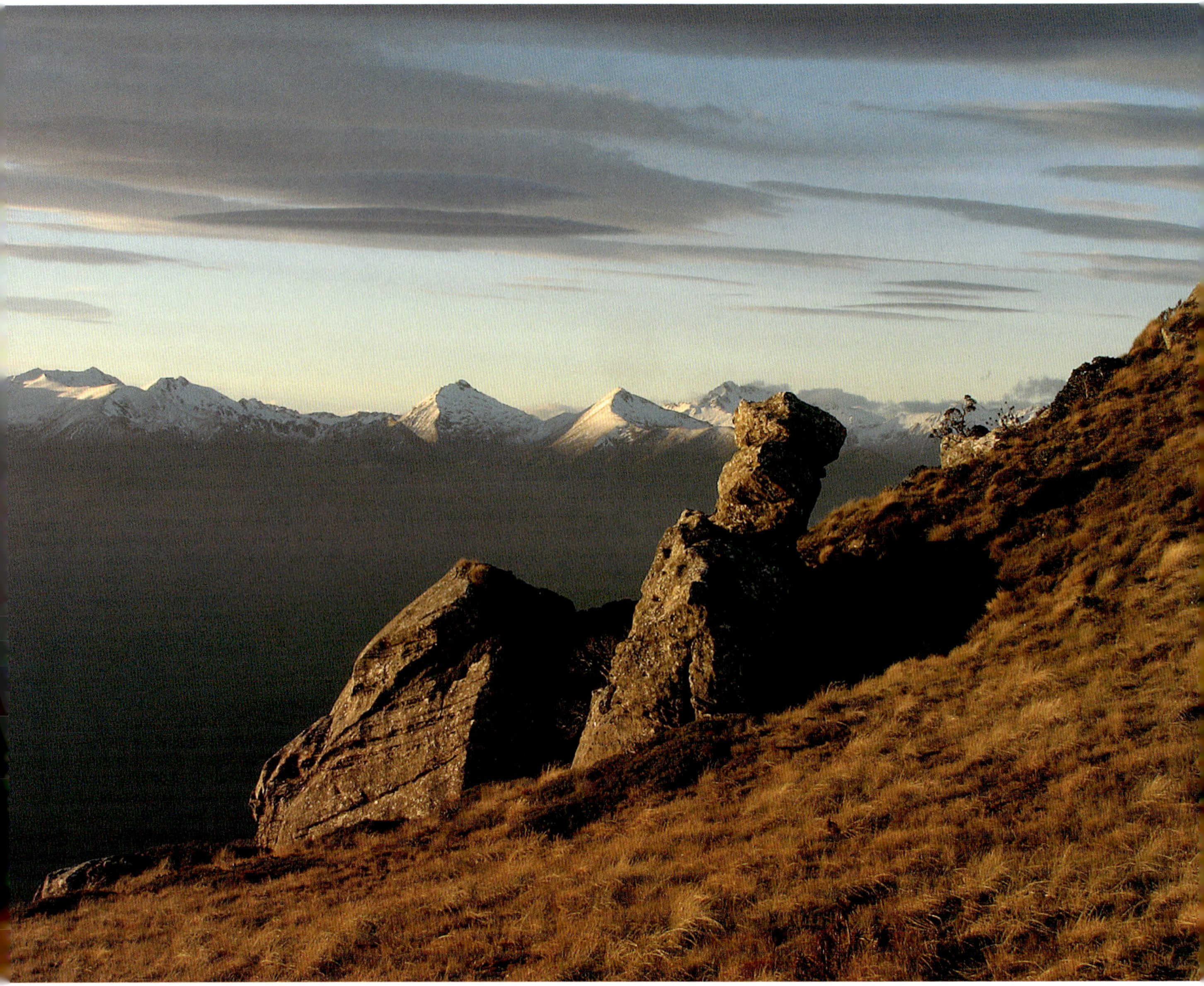

ON NATURE'S EDGE
HUMP RIDGE TRACK, TUATAPERE, SOUTHLAND

On Mussel Beach at Port Craig in south-east Fiordland a rusty boiler and skeletal stumps of an old wharf may seem mute testimony not just to decay but a certain finality and the death of dreams. The 200 people who left from the wharf on 8 October 1928, just three days after it was decided to pull the plug on the largest and most modern sawmill in the country, surely thought so when they turned their back on the ambitious project.

But they were wrong, and today those Port Craig ruins, with the summits of Hump Ridge on the distant skyline and the sands of Te Waewae Bay can be viewed as a symbol of resilience and renewal. And there is no clearer example of such traits than the 53 kilometre Tuatapere Hump Ridge Track, a three-day tramp that is a distinctive blend of bush, beach and subalpine flora that no other national walk offers. The tramp from our southernmost coast to the tundra tops of Hump Ridge and back, through virgin stands of giant southern beech and rimu, can become more than just a walk however. Give way to its history and you'll find it drags at your muddy boots until the posted walking times are irrelevant and anxious hut wardens will lace up their own boots and set off down the trail to see what has become of you.

The catharsis—for that is what it becomes—begins in the former timber milling town of Tuatapere, the sort of place that was actually expected to wither in the brave new world of 1980s economic reform. By rights, the remote town that once served 32 sawmills had no purpose once the chainsaws were finally silenced and the fight to save the last native forests of western Southland was won. Fortunately the economic ideologues seem unable to factor in the feelings of human beings.

Okay, so it is not Auckland's Viaduct Harbour but it is not declining either. A clever tourism marketing strategy came up with the notion of calling the road that traverses the southern coastline from Dunedin to Invercargill before turning, at Tuatapere, north to Te Anau the 'Southern Scenic Route.' Tuatapere, 86 kilometres from Invercargill and 98 kilometres from Te Anau, is a watering hole along the way that, with thoroughly acceptable hyperbole, bills itself as being 'On Nature's Edge.'

And then there is the Tuatapere Hump Ridge Track, a privately operated independent walk on public land that was opened in 2001 and has been a roaring success ever since. The track's origins began in 1991 when 22 outdoors people jumped into kayaks at the head of the Wairaurahiri River on Lake Hauroko and began a rapid descent through

Limestone tors on Hump Ridge (left) appear like nature's version of Easter Island statues.

202 HUMP RIDGE TRACK, TUATAPERE, SOUTHLAND

the Waitutu Forest to the sea. From there, competitors in the inaugural Tuatapere Wild Challenge ran along the old logging tramline, past Port Craig, to Bluecliffs Beach and then rode mountain bikes into Tuatapere. The event, which ran successfully for several years, drew national media coverage and positive national exposure for eastern Fiordland.

In Tuatapere the volunteers and business folk who put in thousands of cumulative hours organising the Wild Challenge were emboldened with confidence at what a determined community could do, particularly one sitting 'on nature's edge.' Creating what amounts to a private track over public land was an ambitious undertaking. But the promoters got a concession to manage a section of the conservation estate, as well as some sympathy for the plight of a community struggling because the native trees it had previously relied on were now locked up in that same estate.

The track proper starts at Rarakau Farm, where a deer fence enclosure next to the homestead keeps cars safe while their owners walk the track. The first half hour of the track is cut through the farm before dropping down to the beach. From here you can follow the remains of an old coastal road or walk along the beach for the next 3 kilometres until the four-wheel-drive road runs out at Track Burn, just outside the Fiordland National Park boundary.

This is the South Coast Track, which follows the coast to the Wairaurahiri River mouth, on through the Waitutu Forest to Big River. In 1896 the Government had a track cut around the coast to serve a short-lived gold-mining operation at Preservation Inlet. A telephone line was slung from tree to tree alongside the track to the Puysegur Point lighthouse until a radio link replaced the line in 1925. The trail that line-maintenance workers strode for more than 40 years remains, however.

Alpine flora and fauna— (anti-clockwise from top left) mountain buttercups, dracophyllum, tomtit and kea—thrive on the heights of Hump Ridge. The trail is well marked through the lower forest (top right) with extensive boardwalking around the tarns and sensitive alpine herb fields on Hump Ridge (centre and bottom).

On this section, once the supply road into Port Craig, it is a wide and well-maintained, Department of Conservation metal walking track. The Hump Ridge looms above the coast, a bush-clad line not too far inland that runs parallel to the western half of Te Waewae Bay. From Track Burn a trail crosses the Ridge to the Teal Bay Hut at Lake Hauroko. But further south on the ridge is a small area of spectacular sandstone tors, alpine tarns, herbfields and views from the Takitimu Mountains to Stewart Island.

It is a spot that inspired Tuatapere's enterprising and determined citizens, who blazed their 'private' track through the coastal beech forest, which is about the easiest tramping you will find. The only surface that is perhaps easier to stride along is the extensive boardwalk pathway, although it has not been laid for tramper comfort. The very features that make the Waitutu so special make it vulnerable to marching feet.

The coastal fringe is a series of 10 terraces that stretch 12 kilometres inland and rise to 650 metres like a giant staircase. They drain poorly and, under the fierce Fiordland rainfall, the forest detritus becomes a sponge, the terraces a series of sodden paddy fields that trampers seeking a drier patch here and there would soon turn into a quagmire. When the boardwalks run out it is a sign that the three-hour grunt to Okaka Lodge, at 928 metres among subalpine tussock, is about to begin. Trail notes advise you to fill your water bottle at the last stream before the climb and it is as well to do so.

Okaka Lodge nestles in the lee of Hump Ridge with sweeping views of Te Waewae Bay. It sleeps 40 in bunk rooms of eight and double or twin bedrooms. Electric lights are powered by a solar-charged system, the toilets flush and the diningroom is huge and comfortable. There is a spacious kitchen with ample gas-powered cookers. Above the hut is a boardwalk circuit around the tors and alpine tarns. Lake Hauroko is on one side, Te Waewae Bay on the other.

Tors and tarns are the dominant features on Hump Ridge. A lookout near Okaka Lodge (left) provides sweeping views of Te Waewae Bay.

Day two is an 18 kilometre, supposedly nine-hour, downhill doddle, down the tongue of the Hump Ridge and the adjoining marine terraces to the coast and then east to Port Craig. But as all trampers know, every downhill involves a fair bit of uphill along the way, and this section is no different, at least until you reach the old railway line and the Edwin Burn Viaduct. It was one of several built along the line by the Marlborough Timber Company to haul logs to its Port Craig mill. The largest, the Percy Burn Viaduct, built in 1925, is 126 metres long and, at 36 metres high, is the highest surviving timber trestle bridge in the world. It was restored in 1994.

When the onset of the Depression closed the Port Craig mill, a team was sent in to recover what it could. They

HUMP RIDGE TRACK, TUATAPERE, SOUTHLAND

HUMP RIDGE TRACK, TUATAPERE, SOUTHLAND

took out 1000 tonnes from the sawmill site and lifted 1000 tonnes of rail lines. The sleepers and the spikes that held the rails are still there.

At Port Craig the old school is restored as a DOC hut, and outside clumps of freesias flower in spring. The Hump Ridge Track Lodge, a little further on, is a twin of the Okaka Lodge, except that hut wardens over the years have decorated it with a few distinctive touches, such as sculptures of driftwood and paua shell. Port Craig is an inviting spot where you could happily linger for one or two days, exploring and absorbing its history. It was economically fated, yet the industry that began in 1916 with the world at war was stunning in its vigour. When it was all over, mill worker John Wakefield wrote in his paybook: 'Finished up. Mill closed down. Here endeth happy days at Port Craig.' Well not for Hump Ridge Track walkers.

Day three is a comfortable 17 kilometre stroll along the coast back to the track start at Rarakau. Until you reach Track Burn and the national park boundary, it is a continuation—actually the first section—of DOC's South Coast Track that you joined on day two. On the beach at Whata are blocks of mudstone embedded with fossil shells that were buried a million years ago and have now resurfaced. And out in the surf you may be lucky enough to spot Hector's dolphins. The track passes through pockets of native bush as well as along the beach for some sections. Keep an eye out for birdlife, deer, seals and penguins. From Track Burn you are on familiar ground and back at Rarakau Farm five to seven hours after leaving Port Craig.

Time Three days, two nights
Length 53 kilometres
Type Bush, subalpine, coastal
Start/finish Rarakau car park, near Tuatapere
Catering On guided option
Pack carry On request
Special features Unsurpassed variety
Party number No limit
Accommodation Modern, fully featured lodges at Okaka and Port Craig village
Bedding Linen provided if required
Season All year
Further information www.humpridgetrack.co.nz

Along the first—and last—section of the track you can walk along the bed of an old tramway or follow the beach and have an opportunity to see the rare Hector's dolphin (left).

The Percy Burn viaduct (p. 206), the highest surviving wooden trestle bridge in the world, was built in 1925 for the logging railway and restored in 1994. Some 1000 tonnes of rail line were lifted with the closure of the Port Craig Mill but most of the sleepers still lie just beneath the mud on the old bush rail line (p. 207), now part of the South Coast Track to Big River.